Empower

Empower

A Guide for Supervisor-Mentors in Theological Field Education

Edited by John Senior and Matthew Floding

An Alban Institute Book

ROWMAN & LITTLEFIELD
Lanham • Boulder • New York • London

Published by Rowman & Littlefield
An imprint of The Rowman & Littlefield Publishing Group, Inc.
4501 Forbes Boulevard, Suite 200, Lanham, Maryland 20706
www.rowman.com

6 Tinworth Street, London SE11 5AL, United Kingdom

British Library Cataloguing in Publication Information Available

Library of Congress Cataloging-in-Publication Data

Names: Floding, Matthew, 1955- editor. | Senior, John, 1971- editor.
Title: Empower : a guide for supervisor-mentors in theological field education / edited by Matthew
    Floding and John Senior.
Description: Lanham : Rowman & Littlefield, [2020] | Series: Explorations in theological field
    education | "An Alban Institute Book." | Includes bibliographical references and index. | Sum-
    mary: "Empower is a guide for supervisor-mentors working with students in ministry internship
    placements and for those who wish to deepen and expand the craft of mentoring in ministry.
    Chapters from experienced ministry mentors provide guidance and support on specific topics
    such as mentoring across cultural differences and facing difficult situations"-- Provided by
    publisher.
Identifiers: LCCN 2020031099 (print) | LCCN 2020031100 (ebook) | ISBN 9781538129111 (cloth :
    alk. paper) | ISBN 9781538129128 (pbk : alk. paper) | ISBN 9781538129135 (electronic)
Subjects: LCSH: Pastoral theology--Fieldwork. | Clergy--Training of. | Mentoring--Religious as-
    pects--Christianity.
Classification: LCC BV4164.5 .E66 2020 (print) | LCC BV4164.5 (ebook) | DDC 253.071/55--dc23
LC record available at https://lccn.loc.gov/2020031099
LC ebook record available at https://lccn.loc.gov/2020031100

♾ ™ The paper used in this publication meets the minimum requirements of American
National Standard for Information Sciences Permanence of Paper for Printed Library
Materials, ANSI/NISO Z39.48-1992.

Contents

Introduction

John Senior

Welcome, mentors of emerging ministry leaders!

This volume is addressed to you, supervisor-mentors of ministry internship placements. Its aim is to provide you with a "tool kit" to aid your work of mentoring student interns. The tool kit metaphor signals our intention to offer concrete resources and strategies for the work of mentoring in theological field education programs. A range of literature explores biblical, theological, sociological, and intersectional frames of mentoring for theological education.[1]

This volume allows other resources to set the broader frameworks for mentoring in theological education. Instead, it attends to the question of how these frameworks might be operationalized in concrete practices and strategies for mentoring emerging ministry leaders. The goal of this book, then, is to help you be better positioned to provide good mentoring, rooted in your wisdom and experience, to students who are on their own vocational journey.

Definitions of mentoring abound. Most note the dynamic of shared wisdom between a seasoned person and a novice. Many also identify that while a primary aim of mentoring is to support and advance the more novice partner in his development (personal, professional, spiritual, etc.), good mentoring also has the effect of enriching both parties in a number of different ways. I love the way Pamela Holliman distills her understanding of mentoring into one phrase: "self-conscious wisdom."[2] That phrase packs in a lot. In this introduction, I would like to consider what mentoring as self-conscious wisdom means for the development of ministry leaders in field education placements—especially in the context of a dramatically "shifting ecclesial landscape," to use a now-familiar phrase. Ecclesial institutions have been and continue to be containers of wisdom about the life and work of ministry. As the shapes of these institutions change, mentoring as self-conscious wisdom for emerging ministry leaders is more vital now than ever.

Many have suggested that ministry is all about wisdom. To say that ministry is about wisdom is to say something about what ministers know about their craft and how they know it. I find the distinction that ancient thinkers made between different kinds of knowledge to be helpful here. Good ministry is not rooted in technical knowledge, as if it could happen through the reading and implementation of how-to instruction manuals or cookbooks.[3]

Neither is wise ministry formed through the exploration and analysis of elegant theories about ministry that hover high above the messiness and complexity of real human lives. Although both technical know-how and theoretical analysis are important ingredients of wisdom, wisdom is something different than both. Wisdom arises in and through experience and, in particular, through intentional reflection on experience in ways that operationalize technical, theoretical, and other forms of knowledge. Wisdom happens when the messiness of experience both fills out and complicates but also receives instruction and guidance from technical, theoretical, embodied, and other ways of knowing. In operationalizing multiple ways of knowing in conversation with experience, wise ministers arrive at a fitting response to a particular situation, in a particular moment in time, involving particular people who exist in a particular context. Wisdom as knowledge of the fitting is what the Greeks called *phronesis*.

Here's the critical question for you, the mentor: how do persons learn *phronesis*—that is, how do persons learn to operationalize multiple kinds of knowledge to form judgments about real experiences in ways that reflect and generate wisdom? This is where you come into play. Wisdom is learned through experience combined with intentional reflection on experience, in conversation with persons who have been "down that road" and, therefore, know something about what they are doing. Drawing on your own experience and wisdom, you, the skillful mentor, invite mentees, often through posing powerful questions, to consider a range of factors that contribute to a mentee's growth. These questions might include:

• How does an awareness of oneself shape the way one practices ministry and understands oneself as a minister?
• How does my formation in my family and communities of origin, important life experiences, significant relationships, and so forth, inform one's presence and practice of ministry?
• How does a thoughtful analysis of context inform ministry with others?
• What does this ministry experience tell me about which strategies for effective ministry tend to work and which ones don't?

- What does it teach me about the ways in which God is calling me to ministry?
- Where is God present and working in my life and ministry experiences?

In occasioning reflection around these and other themes, mentors help mentees to operationalize multiple forms of knowledge to make meaning of their experience. Mentors, in other words, are necessary catalysts for wisdom.

Not all wisdom is "self-conscious" in the sense of immediate, critical awareness. Wisdom often is deeply embodied, a kind of "second nature," and thus semiconscious or perhaps even preconscious.[4] In mentoring, as Holliman says, the wisdom of both mentor and mentee becomes self-conscious. That process of raising wisdom to awareness is much easier said than done. Good mentors recognize that mentees already have some of the experiential building blocks of wisdom about the life and work of ministry, though that wisdom may not yet be self-conscious. The challenge for the mentor is to use her own wisdom in order to invite mentees to bring their emerging wisdom to self-consciousness. The wisdom of the mentor invites the wisdom of the mentee to emerge into self-consciousness. Once brought to awareness, wisdom can be explored, deepened, nuanced, and better positioned to inform continuing practice.

That's different than saying that the mentor uses his wisdom to shape the mentee, as though the job of the mentor is to mold the mentee in the mentor's own image. One might imagine that in some contexts, mentoring is more like a kind of molding in the form of the seasoned professional. The military, for example, might require a form of mentoring that shapes military professionals to a mold, in order to ensure the proper, uniform functioning of military units.

But mentoring for ministry is different. Good mentoring for ministry is not about shaping the mentee after the image of the mentor. It does not look like a series of monologues, delivered by the mentor, in which the mentor dispenses her wisdom to the mentee. Rather, good mentors leverage their wisdom in order to further the mentee's journey, not the mentor's journey. In doing so, mentors inevitably learn something about their own journey along the way. This leveraging of the mentor's wisdom in ways that open up the mentee's vocational journey is at the core of the work of mentoring.

If one problematic approach to mentoring is the rigid strategy of making one's mentee over in one's own image, the polar opposite is offering the mentee no structure or guidance at all. One of our veteran supervisor-mentors recounts a summer ministry internship experience in South America. This person's mentor in that context offered very little intentional supervision or mentoring. The student rightly felt lost in the ministry internship experience. At the end of the summer, the supervisor-mentor gave this person a poor assessment of the summer's internship work. In a way, this person says, the "mentor" was right: the student had no guidance, and as a result, the student mostly missed the mark in his work. Perhaps the mentor thought it was important for the student to be thrown into the work and figure it out for himself, to "sink or swim." The problem here is that without a wise conversation partner, the student's emerging wisdom went unprocessed. It did not rise to the level of "self-consciousness" and thus was not made useful to the mentee as he continued to learn about ministry in that particular setting. At the same time, the mentor did not benefit from the insights that a student may offer about the ministry he shared with the mentor, nor did the mentor have the opportunity to reflect on his own continued growth through generative conversations with the mentee.

Good mentors neither attempt to make mentees over in their own image, nor do they abandon mentees to experience internship work all on their own. Instead, good mentors strike a delicate balance between, on the one hand, helping mentees create clear, goal-driven structures that promote accountability for learning in the internship experience, and, on the other, creating space for the mentee to develop her own identity, presence, and sense of purpose as an emerging ministry leader.

The ability to strike a generative balance between structure and openness is itself a kind of wisdom that mentors cultivate through experience. The key question for you here is: how can I operationalize my wisdom and experience in ways that promote the student's growth on *his* journey in ministry (as opposed to my own journey)? This is difficult discernment. Shadowing, for example, can be a useful mentoring strategy, particularly for an inexperienced student at the outset of an internship placement. But a shadowing process, at a certain point, can crowd out space for the student to experience himself as a minister—to learn, in other words, how he would do the work of ministry in ways that align with his own gifts, character, dispositions, and so forth. Our mentors often report that they find it difficult to let go of control, or at least of their perception of control, of leadership in their ministry setting in order to make space for interns to lead. This is, in part, because mentors rightly are anxious about their perception that ultimately the "buck stops" with them on matters of leadership in their context. Similarly, our mentors struggle to discern when it is appropriate to allow a student to fail in situations when the mentor can see a problem unfolding several steps before it reaches fruition.

I hear our mentors often reporting on the wisdom they have developed around striking this balance. For example, a mentor in our program has made a practice of having an initial conversation with his ministry interns about the family system dynamics and, in particular, the individuals in his congregation who tend to determine those dynamics. This mentor, however, makes a point of not saying too much about his own interactions with these individuals or the strategies he has developed for engaging them. That way, his interns do not feel blindsided by system dynamics, and, at the same time, students do not feel responsible for or accountable to the mentor's experiences with these persons. The student is better positioned to navigate these dynamics in her own way.

In my view, the practice of discernment is at the heart of the work of ministry, and it is also at the heart of wise mentoring. By "discernment" here, I mean a disposition of continual openness to God's voice and call, both in one's own life and in the life of the communities that one serves. Mentors steeped in practices of discernment are not likely to be inclined to make mentees over in their own image because they know that they themselves are not finished products. Mentoring as conformation to a stable model doesn't make sense when the mentor knows the model isn't entirely stable.

Although they have important lessons to teach about ministry, these mentors also know that God is calling the mentee to be the mentee, not the mentor. In his book *Let Your Life Speak*, Parker Palmer recounts a famous "Hasidic tale" that, he says, "reveals, with amazing brevity, both the universal tendency to want to be someone else and the ultimate importance of becoming one's self: Rabbi Zusya, when he was an old man, said, 'In the coming world, they will not ask me: "Why were you not Moses?" They will ask me: "Why were you not Zusya?"'"[5] In a posture of continuing discernment, wise mentors orient themselves around this question: how can I help this mentee become more of himself as I also become more of myself in the process?

There is a way that our ecclesial institutions carry ministry wisdom in their traditions, practices, and even in their built environment. One has a pretty good idea, for example, of the kind of homiletic performance that is supposed to issue from a raised mahogany pulpit in an old New England sanctuary. We are very aware at the moment how quickly and dramatically many of our ecclesial institutions are changing, as are the patterns, practices, and traditions that made them what they are. This is probably a good thing in many ways—but the fact that our institutions are so unsettled disrupts the wisdom about the practice of ministry that they have carried.

If, for example, the formal homiletic traditionally at home in the raised pulpits of old New England churches no longer resonates culturally, how is the wisdom associated with this particular kind of homiletic practice meaningful? This is why discernment as a practice of ministry is so critical. Ministry leaders continually have to be attuned to the new ways in which God is calling their communities to practice ministry. That attunement also should inform the mentoring of emerging ministry leaders. Good mentoring in the current moment will demonstrate a commitment not only to the learning of emerging ministry leaders, but also to the continual learning of the church as its institutional shape continues to change.[6] Continuing discernment about the latter should motivate and energize the work of discernment for the former.

This book is organized in four sections, each exploring a theme designed to offer concrete wisdom about the practices of mentoring ministry interns. These three broad themes are separated artificially for the purposes of organizing this volume intelligibly. In reality, of course, these themes intersect and modulate one another in complex ways.

Section I ("Mentoring for Ministry Essentials") explores mentoring strategies around what loosely might be called "foundational" habits and dispositions for ministry—foundational in the sense that these habits and dispositions lend distinctiveness to ministry as a vocation, while also sustaining the work of ministry in any context in which ministry leaders might serve. The work of continuing discernment, spiritual development, theological reflection, cultivating resilience, drawing and keeping professional boundaries, developing life-giving peer relationships, practicing ministry ethics, and developing cultural humility all are vital to the life and work of ministry across career and context.

Section II ("Mentoring for Ministry in Context") turns to the work of mentoring in relation to context-specific issues and themes: mentoring for engagement with diverse ministry settings, relational systems, and identities and experiences.[7]

Section III ("Mentoring for Leadership Formation") offers perspectives on mentoring around specific ministry leadership roles and practices. We hope that readers will find insight and wisdom in the intersecting conversations that this volume offers.

We also hope that this "tool kit" offers you concrete approaches to the work of mentoring ministry interns around a range of themes, while also encouraging you to rely on your own emerging and deepening wisdom about the work of mentoring. Your mentoring work is absolutely critical in the process of vocational formation that our ministry students experience as they prepare for ministry. For your critical contributions to that process, we are deeply grateful.

We want to thank our contributors for their thoughtful and wise contributions to this volume. We also want to thank Rolf Janke, Natalie Mandziuk, Brianna Westervelt, and others at Rowman & Littlefield for their dedication to this project and for working with us to bring it to life. Finally, we thank Hilary Floyd, doctoral student in Bible and Cultures at Drew University, for her careful editing of the volume and for preparing the index.

I

Mentoring for Ministry Essentials

Chapter One

Mentoring Ethically

Catherine M. Brall

When a seasoned pastor remarked, "Being a field education supervisor is hard work," I responded quickly with, "But it's also *good* work." Part of what makes good (and challenging) work is reflecting critically on the nature and boundaries of what is "good" (and perhaps not so good), not only in terms of the ministry situations your students may bring to you, but also in terms of the mentor-student relationship. Discussions that center on discerning what is good and what one should do in the teaching, practice, and supervision of ministry are rooted in the ethics of ministry. Ministerial ethics generally have not received the same amount of attention as those of other professions including medicine, business, and law.[1]

Richard Gula remarks, "As a general rule, ministers, unlike many other professionals, have no code of ethics to which they can turn for support or guidance."[2] Some think this lack of attention to a formal code of ethics stems from the assumption that as people of faith, you are good, moral persons and will act accordingly. Barbara Blodgett asserts the importance of ethics for ministry because there is a deep yearning for trust and authenticity that people seek from their clergy, that clergy aspire to in their own vocations, and that faith communities desire corporately.[3]

Both Blodgett and Gula develop ethical principles for ministry from the foundation of various biblical covenants established throughout scripture. Covenants share similar features with contracts but differ with regard to the spirit of the arrangements. Whereas contracts clearly delineate expectations and responsibilities of the parties involved, establishing boundaries and setting limitations, covenants express similar components in more flexible and gracious ways, focusing on keeping the parties in healthy and mutually beneficial relationships with each other.

Most field education programs require that you and your students work out a Learning/Serving Covenant[4] to articulate learning goals for your work together and to define other parameters that govern your relationship. This document intentionally bears the name "covenant" to convey God's centrality to the work that you both will undertake. Over the course of your time together, you likely will experience some moments of great grace and perhaps even glorious transcendence, along with those other occasions when confusion, frustration, and conflict seem to reign. All of these moments afford you opportunities for transformation and growth as a supervisor, minister, and most important, beloved child of God. Good supervision functions a bit like poetry in its nuanced communication of the affective, aesthetic, and theological aspects that accompany the concrete elements of ministerial activities.[5]

As you embark on this sacred work of mentoring ministers in formation, consider the paraphrase below of the familiar injunction from Micah 6:8:

> God has shown you, O Supervisor/Mentor, what is good and what is required
> of you: Do justice, love mercy, and walk humbly with your God.

Methods to incorporate these three basic commands as a set of lenses to examine your interactions, discern your motivations, recognize your preconceptions, and propose alternatives to enable more ethical mentoring for your interns follow. Nothing here likely will be new or surprising, but it's offered to help you recall lessons learned for your students' benefit.

DOING JUSTICE

What might it mean to "do justice" as you supervise and mentor your students? This key biblical concept calls God's people to respond to God's grace toward them by engaging in true religion—an ethical response that includes not only personal and communal righteousness, but manifests itself in broader, social dimensions. Practically, doing justice includes being fair and equitable with an awareness of acting in ways that are proper, fitting, true to the spirit, and without partiality in executing the learning/serving covenant you have made. No doubt, you have every intention to treat your seminarians justly. In the challenges of real-world ministry, the following temptations to be less than your best self may surface.

One way to begin compromising on what is right for you to expect from your seminarians is to lose perspective of the power differential between the two of you. You have much more power than your interns because several factors contribute cumulatively to the unequal power dynamics. Your mentor role expects you to evaluate and report to the seminary and/or the ordaining judicatory your assessment of strengths, weaknesses, skills, maturity, and character of your students at certain points in the field experience. You have more experience in ministry and hold a significant level of authority at the placement site to be qualified to supervise. Your attitude toward the students' abilities strongly influences how others at the site relate to them.

Avoid taking advantage of the power differential such that you "use" them in ways that go beyond the expectations of the relationship. Allowing your seminarians to respond appropriately to unexpected events and genuine emergencies such as substituting for Sunday school or leading part of the worship with little notice may offer beneficial insights into their gifts and coping skills. However, when the "unexpected emergency" becomes the routine, the failure on your part to address systemic, structural issues places your interns in an unfair position and may compromise the effectiveness of the learning environment. Obvious inappropriate requests including babysitting or running personal errands often begin on a mundane and acceptable level. Real-life pressures can lead supervisors and students down the slippery slope of progressive boundary violations that eventually may appear to be justifiable or even beneficial for all parties. The best practice is to avoid entertaining such scenarios.

In beginning the mentoring relationship, take time to reflect and effectively communicate how you will exercise your supervisory role. Discuss the primary goal(s) of your supervisory relationship (i.e., accomplishing work, helping students to clarify issues, reflecting theologically, developing pastoral relationships, teaching skills, etc.) as well as the tasks that you intend to undertake toward these goals such as assigning work, maintaining accountability, and nurturing self-awareness. Describe the scope of the supervision, including anticipated work at the site; methodology of how you engage in work; and issues, goals, and problems of the seminarian. Disclose when and how you are likely to assess the students' work and who else in the organization may have input into those evaluations. In this discussion, ask your students to reflect about past supervisory experiences and share honestly about helpful and ineffective experiences. Your ability to encourage your students' reflections and listen carefully to what is shared will empower your students and reduce the stressful dynamics in play due to the power differential.

It's wise for you to avoid dual relationships and the role confusion that comes with them. Practically speaking, you shouldn't be a pastor and/or a spiritual director to students as well a supervisor-mentor because expectations for how students should be supported and challenged differ in each configuration. For example, it wouldn't be fair to the privileged nature of a spiritual direction relationship to subsequently have to evaluate students' abilities in leading public prayer as a field mentor. More subtly, your impartiality can be skewed by having friendships, professional relationships, or a history of substantial interactions with members of students' family. Maintaining good boundaries, keeping confidences within multiple layers of relationships, and being aware of how such circumstances can influence your supervision will help you deal justly with your interns.

Last, it's essential to honor the scheduling, time commitments, and other promises you've made explicitly or implicitly to your seminarians. In supervisory sessions, give your students your full attention. Remember that how you model good supervision with your students will influence their likelihood to do the same with their future subordinates. Silence your phone, turn off instant messaging, and meet in a space where you are less likely to be disturbed and that permits privacy to converse deeply and fully. For example, one supervisor-mentor takes interns to a local coffee shop for their supervisory sessions to reduce staff interruptions and the tendency of parishioners to drop by when they see her car in the church's lot. Additional ways to diminish interruptions such as posting a "Do Not Disturb" sign on the office door may be found.

LOVING MERCY

In the Micah 6:8 verse, the loving "mercy" is a translation of the Hebrew verb *chesed*, which primarily describes God's actions and attitude toward God's people. The word is translated as loving-kindness, mercy, goodness, kindness, loyalty, and love, with the emphasis being on the steadfast, committed love God has for humanity and demonstrating God's faithfulness in keeping the covenantal relationships God establishes. God's example may inspire you to stay faithful to the spirit of *chesed* in your covenantal commitments to your students.

First, acting with love means supervising them in ways that seek to maximize their benefit and seek to prevent and lessen any harm from your words, actions, and those of others within your direct sphere of influence and control. Such intentions and actions are at the center of mentoring ethically. Being trustworthy in your pastoral interactions demonstrates this love and is essential not only in direct encounters with your interns, but in all interactions that you model for your seminarians. As your students observe and participate with you in various aspects of ministry, share the processes of discernment that guide specific actions you take or refrain from taking. Discuss the importance of recognizing that just because you can do something, doesn't mean that you should do it. Acting ethically means carefully evaluating the costs and benefits involved in taking or declining any action. Engaging these thought processes with students helps them grasp the intuitive dynamics that compose the experienced ministers' "pastoral imagination."

Be aware of the inherent tensions involved in training and modeling certain roles and ministry skills for your students. On the one hand, it is necessary to give your students sufficient guidance and direction to begin to inhabit these roles with some degree of success. For example, the first time students lead a portion of the liturgy or make a pastoral visit, you may need to direct them closely if they are uncertain about what faithful engagement in the task looks like. On the other hand, loving-kindness dictates that you exercise care to avoid molding students in your image but rather seek to recognize, develop, and affirm your students' unique gifts in undertaking ministry. The more gifted or experienced your seminarians are in any facet of ministry, the more likely they are to engage differently than you would. Supervising in love affirms and delights in these differences.

Many books written about ethics in pastoral ministry devote chapters to the ethical implications of truth telling and keeping confidences.[6] In supervising, it is important to be truthful with your students, yet the command to love mercy asks you to be mindful of how and when you convey information that may be difficult or hurtful to receive. This is especially true with the "tender parts" and vulnerable edges that seminarians new to ministry may expose. Your supervisory observations and conversations may enable you to perceive wounds or deficits in your students that were you to reveal them, more harm than good would result because your interns do not yet have the capacity or resiliency to process the information. Being merciful also suggests that negative feedback be given in a private setting when the conditions allow for the information to be communicated and processed in a supportive way.

Serving as a field education supervisor-mentor may require you to evaluate your students and share your observations and assessment with their educational institution or judicatory. Otherwise, keep them confidential. Likewise, personal details of the students' background and experiences shared during supervisory sessions, particularly embarrassing ones, are best kept confidential unless a situation arises for mandated reporting. If you have questions about what information should be shared and with whom to benefit your students, consult with the field education director at your students' school. Field educators are equipped to facilitate the mutual interests you and your students bring to such matters.

Maintaining loving-kindness toward your students may be most difficult when they make mistakes, upset people with power in your setting, or instigate situations that reflect poorly on your leadership and mentoring skills. As a supervisor-mentor seeking to love mercy, you would acknowledge and stay faithful to the relationship with your seminarians and to the learning covenant, earnestly attempting sympathy toward your students' sincere efforts and empathy with your students' personhood as a minister-in-formation. Nonetheless, hold your students accountable for their part in the situation, allowing them to bear some consequences as will be helpful for learning and reinforcing past lessons. Being merciful does not permit you to ignore or enable your students' bad behavior, uncritical thinking, and abdication of responsibility. Doing so would harm your students' formation, and therefore, be unhelpful and unethical.

WALKING HUMBLY WITH GOD

This final command of Micah 6:8 presents the greatest challenge for transla-tors in that the biblical word used for "humbly" appears only here in the Hebrew Bible. The most common translations of this unique word "humbly" include modestly, circumspectly, prudently, thoughtfully, and wisely. The command invites you to remember that your supervision is done in fellow-ship with and, ultimately, under the guidance and direction of God. Your work as a mentor will also form and mentor you if you approach it with humility and an open heart and mind.

As you meet for theological reflection with your students, be mindful to model through your words and attitude your recognition that the power and authority you have as a leader is subservient to the reign of God in your life and ministry. Discuss with your seminarians your processes for discerning how your actions and decisions seek to work cooperatively with the activity of God in situations and in keeping with God's character. Your interns may benefit from hearing about occasions when you forgot about walking humbly with God and ran headstrong after the agenda of your ego and of pleasing the desires of other humans. In sharing your negative examples, highlight how God's faithfulness manifested itself to resolve your difficulties, directly through the work of the Holy Spirit or through the intervention of others. In contrast, if your stories primarily relate how your wisdom, merit, and strength saved the day, you are modeling narcissism in place of humble discipleship. Commit to regularly pray for the formation and development of your students and also pray for yourself in this important ministry of supervi-sion. In the spirit of true humility, you also may appropriately share some of your needs with your students, requesting their prayers.

One final aspect of walking humbly with God is shown through your recognition of the limits of your own knowledge and skills in response to various ministry demands. Certainly, in pastoral counseling, you have an ethical responsibility to refer people who need more expert care than you can provide. Let your students see you seeking counsel from those within your context who have more knowledge, skills, or other resources to address the issue at hand. Model the sharing of leadership burdens and delegating certain tasks and responsibilities to capable others. Your students will benefit from having a more realistic understanding of healthy leadership if you are not the primary rescuer in your organization. Walking humbly does not mean walk-ing alone, but rather journeying in compassionate companionship with others toward the call and mission God has given. Mentoring your students in a healthy community where doing justice and loving mercy are embodied will sow seeds of virtue and bear much fruit in their future ministry.

QUESTIONS FOR REFLECTION

1. Which of the three commands—doing justice, loving mercy, and walking humbly with God—were most apparent in the mentors you had in your formation and early ministry experiences? How will these influences shape your practices as a supervisor-mentor?
2. In an article written for interns, Barbara Blodgett tells them, "As an intern, you are in the business of giving and receiving trust. Therefore, you should prioritize trust over the giving and receiving of anything else."[7] As you recall your own experiences of being a field education student or intern, what did you tend to prioritize from that time in your formation? Why?
3. What are your priorities now as you strive to be ethical in your mentoring relationships with your interns? How and why have these priorities changed over time for you? How might they be shaped by the needs of the students you're supervising?

SUGGESTED READINGS

Blodgett, Barbara J. "Ministerial Ethics." In *Welcome to Theological Field Education!*, edited by Matthew Floding. Lanham, MD: Rowman & Littlefield, 2011.

Bush, Joseph E., Jr. *Gentle Shepherding: Pastoral Ethics and Leadership.* Atlanta, GA: Chalice Press, 2006.

Gula, Richard M. *Ethics in Pastoral Ministry.* Mahwah, NJ: Paulist Press, 1996.

Weist, Walter E., and Elwyn A. Smith. *Ethics in Ministry: A Guide for the Professional.* Minneapolis, MN: Fortress Press, 1990.

Chapter Two

Mentoring for Vocational Discernment

Stephanie Crumley-Effinger

WHY IS DISCERNMENT NEEDED?

Students come to seminary with a diverse range of gifts and callings to ministry. Long gone are the days when the purpose of theological education was to prepare everyone for pastoral ministry or religious education in a congregational setting. As a result, you are invited to look and listen deeply for the gifts for ministry within your students. God is indeed doing new things and calls us to respond creatively to the brisk winds of the Spirit blowing within, through, and beyond seminaries, congregations, and other religious organizations and structures. As a mentor you can nurture your students in discovering or imagining opportunities for using their gifts both now and in the years to come. Given the changes in religious life and contemporary society, this likely will occur in forms of ministry that do not currently exist or are not yet recognized.

An internship provides particularly valuable opportunities for students to deepen intentional vocational discernment while engaged in ministry. As your students develop and practice skills through learning and serving, you can support them in integrating this new information and set of experiences into their continuing process of discernment. Mentors and peers who journey with students, listening deeply, praying for and with them, and giving feedback on what they observe, can effectively support the student in discernment about how God is at work in their lives and the gifts they bring. Ongoing vocational exploration of ministry also is nurtured by students reading about and observing various forms of gifts and ministry along with prayerfully considering, discussing, and reflecting in writing on what they notice and the feedback they receive.

You can lead your student in exploring and writing about various facets of their giftedness for ministry. Considering gifts (and challenges) arising or developed through life experience, work experience, personality, and spiritual gifts provides students with differing perspectives that overlap, expand, and complement one another, offering a rich array of input to ponder. Your student's understanding can be deepened powerfully through exploring their emerging sense of their gifts and calling as the focus person for a clearness committee.[1] This is a prayerful corporate discernment process in which one is asked centered Spirit-led questions; it is enhanced when followed later by debriefing with a mentor.

I became acquainted with the practice of clearness committees through being a member of the Religious Society of Friends (Quakers), by which they were developed. As Patricia Loring details in the booklet *Spiritual Discernment: The Context and Goal of Clearness Committees*, these originally had a very limited focus, but in modern times they have been adapted for use with many different kinds of questions an individual or group faces.[2] Quaker educator and writer Parker Palmer has introduced the practice of committees for clearness to a wide audience, particularly through his work with the Circle of Trust program through The Center for Courage & Renewal.[3]

ATTITUDES AND PRACTICES TO SUPPORT DISCERNMENT

To provide effective mentoring for discernment, place your trust in God's guiding presence and do not rely on your own efforts. You can cultivate your capacity to attend to Divine leading[4] by intentionally connecting to the Spirit through the regular practice of centering prayer,[5] another kind of contemplation in silence, or more kataphatic forms of meditation such as lectio divina,[6] singing Taizé chants,[7] or reflecting on art.[8]

Nurturing your own spiritual sensitivity will empower you to let go of your own agenda and focus instead on supporting students in such qualities as faithfulness, justice, self-awareness, openness to growth, and being teachable, grounded, courageous, and truthful. Early Quaker leader George Fox taught,

> The Scriptures were the prophets' words and Christ's and the apostles' words, and what they spoke they enjoyed and possessed and had it from the Lord. . . . Then what had any to do with the Scriptures, but as they came to the Spirit that gave them forth. You will say, Christ saith this, and the apostles say this; but what canst thou say? Art thou a child of Light and has walked in Light, and what thou speakest is it inwardly from God?[9]

In addition to investing in your own ongoing preparation, you can focus on a number of time-honored practices and approaches to serve your students in discernment. Listen deeply

> with as complete attentiveness as [you] can muster . . . listen with [your] hearts, the marrow of [your] bones and [your] whole skin, as well as with [your] ears. Such listening is one dimension of the discipline of contemplative prayer. It is also at least as evocative as any question in drawing a speaker past self-definition and limitation, into the more spacious reality of God's will. [10]

Pay close attention to the student's voice, face, hand movements, changes in energy level, and so forth, because these can provide insight and wisdom. You may need to wait patiently, offering gentle hospitality for what might emerge.

> The soul speaks its truth only under quiet, inviting, and trustworthy conditions. [It] is like a wild animal—tough, resilient, savvy, self-sufficient, and yet exceedingly shy. If we want to see a wild animal, the last thing we should do is to go crashing through the woods, shouting for the creature to come out. But if we are willing to walk quietly into the woods and sit silently for an hour or two at the base of the tree, the creature we are waiting for may well emerge, and out of the corner of an eye we will catch a glimpse of the precious wildness we seek. [11]

You can prepare yourself, you can listen well with the Spirit's help, but discernment is grounded in Divine guidance. You can seek God's leadership throughout the conversation—praying for direction as your time together begins and continually opening yourself to Holy assistance as the speaking and listening proceed. A student wrote about putting this into practice when having difficult conversations:

> I began to learn about how and when it was my time to verbalize my ideas. I have a long way to go, but listening to my feelings and the Divine, I can be aware of the proper time to speak . . . I have some new techniques in language, "I see it in a different way, or through a different lens" without putting the other person on the defense.

Listen for and attend to nudges you receive from the Holy Spirit, and ask centered questions as these arise, to help the persons deepen their understanding of whatever they have brought for consideration. Civil rights activist and theologian Ruby Sales described her leading to ask such a question:

> I was getting my locks washed, and my locker's daughter came in one morning, and she had been hustling all night. And she had sores on her body. And she was just in a state—drugs. So something said to me, ask her: "Where does it hurt?" And I said, "Shelley, where does it hurt?" And just that simple

question unleashed territory in her that she had never shared with her mother. And she talked about having been incested. She talked about all of the things that had happened to her as a child. And she literally shared the source of her pain. [12]

Discernment invites faithful response. You can support your student in making incremental movement forward in explorations of direction. "Discernment can be like driving an automobile at night: the headlights cast only enough light for us to see the next small bit of road immediately in front of us." [13] Because the reality is that

> [it] is necessary to live into the fullness of one's Light and discernment even before we have the whole picture. It would be nice to wait until we see how everything fits together. But that is a luxury we cannot wait for. What is required is that we walk in what we know now. In the walking more will be added. In obedience to the discernment we presently have, more discernment will be opened to us. [14]

In this way you can assist your student in making such tentative exploratory steps, encouraging them to "Live up to the Light thou hast and more will be granted thee." [15] A student wrote about this on a year-end self-evaluation:

> my theological supervisor . . . helped me to see many experiences from a different perspective and she always encouraged me to look at these experiences in both a spiritual and practical light. She also helped me to work through the changes I need to make in my life. I had always believed that when God nudged me to do something that I should immediately get started on it but I had a strong resistance to the latest nudge. This nudge was to get out of my safe little cocoon and start living my life differently. My supervisor-mentor helped me to see that I didn't have to make a drastic change. I could take baby steps and still honor God's call.

You can advocate for taking the time needed for a decision or process to ripen, and knowing when to slow down the trajectory. Encourage your student to be patient with themselves and with the process. Reinforce the value of having exploratory conversations without prematurely seeking an answer or commitment. Conversely, some people are more likely to err in the opposite direction—wanting to explore incessantly without ever coming to a decision—and need to be encouraged to learn when it is time to stop exploring and decide.

Another resource for your student's discernment is the wisdom of trustworthy people—not to provide answers, but to support a fruitful process that fosters an answer arising within the students. Such persons can be of great value in asking questions, providing information, identifying possibilities, exploring ideas, or sharing experiences.

In the midst of discernment, continue to reinforce for your student that God provides a reliable plumb line, helping your students connect to Truth as they know it or as you have heard them reference experiencing it. This is especially important to do when they encounter disruptions or new opportunities due to the dynamic nature of life, whether in their internship, friendships, or other places. Such changes often require one to adjust and readjust as is fitting to the movement underway, rather than always stay with a previous decision.

Finally, you can provide the often difficult and uncomfortable service of offering loving challenge to the student you are mentoring. This can include giving feedback that empowers them to acknowledge a limitation they would prefer not to see and supporting them in identifying what else is possible.

> As often happens on the spiritual journey, we have arrived at the heart of a paradox: each time a door closes, the rest of the world opens up. All we need to do is stop pounding on the door that just closed, turn around—which puts the door behind us—and welcome the largeness of life that now lies open to our souls. The door that closed kept us from entering a room, but what now lies before us is the rest of reality. [16]

A faculty member had just such a tenderly truthful conversation with a student who was eager to discuss ideas for an internship. It was painful, but important, for the student to hear that he would need to make meaningful progress in dealing with several issues that have affected his schoolwork negatively before the faculty would feel clear to approve him as ready for an internship. Without this kind of faithful honest feedback, how can any of us engage growth opportunities that we do not apprehend?

Both in this internship, and for faithful life and ministry, your discernment work with your students is invaluable.

QUESTIONS FOR REFLECTION

1. What is your capacity to sit with uncertainty—resisting internal or external pressure to supply an answer or to push another toward what you believe is best for them—and to listen deeply to the other persons and the Holy Spirit together, supporting the interns toward discerning a faithful decision?
2. What practices have you found to deepen and increase your ability to "stop and listen," both to listen for guidance and to listen to another person? To what extent and in what ways do you regularly make use of one or more of these practices?
3. The ability to listen deeply to other people and to the Holy Spirit, and to act on guidance one receives, is a dynamic process in which God

keeps inviting us to increase our capacity; what growth area(s) have arisen recently for your attention, and how are you addressing these?

SUGGESTED READINGS

Bill, J. Brent. *Sacred Compass: The Way of Spiritual Discernment.* Brewster, MA: Paraclete, 2008.

Farnham, Suzanne, Joseph P. Gill, R. Taylor McLean, and Susan M. Ward. *Listening Hearts; Discerning Call in Community.* Harrisburg, PA: Morehouse, 2011.

Lacey, Paul. *Leading and Being Led.* Wallingford, PA: Pendle Hill, 1985.

Loring, Patricia. *Spiritual Discernment: The Context and Goal of Clearness Committees.* Wallingford, PA: Pendle Hill, 1992.

Palmer, Parker. *Let Your Life Speak: Listening for the Voice of Vocation.* San Francisco, CA: Jossey-Bass, 2000.

Chapter Three

Mentoring for Spiritual Development

Geoff Vandermolen

THE IMPORTANCE OF MENTORING FOR SPIRITUAL DEVELOPMENT

As a ministry leader you may have wrestled with this unsettling truth: you will not reach the summit of ministry impact or longevity because of manicured ministry skills, by out-hustling others, or by some unique feature of your theological tradition. You might initially bristle at this statement, but consider it for a minute or two. Most of us live with an awareness that every sermon already has been preached and every pastoral situation already encountered.

So, what do you do? Add a smoke machine to worship? Buy a ministry kit that promises to revitalize discipleship at your church for the low price of $499?

There is another way.

Consider the following statement: *the delightful uniqueness that you and your mentee bring to ministry leadership is the mysterious and inventive way(s) in which the Holy Spirit animates you with your particular gifts, passions, words, sermons, pastoral care, prayers, and overall Kingdom ministry.* What is your internal reaction to this assertion? Does it make you feel fearful? Grateful? Hopeful? Disappointed? Liberated? It is possible that both you and your mentee will dislike this statement. If so, consider spending some time reflecting on the source of your discomfort. Whether in discomfort or uttering an "Amen" to this statement, the most immediate and necessary step in your formation is to get comfortable "living in step with the Spirit of God."[1] In fact, I would argue that you will grow most in ministry effectiveness and joy by engaging in mentoring for spiritual development.

WHAT IS MENTORING FOR SPIRITUAL DEVELOPMENT?

In ministry I have benefited from mentors of various kinds. Some mentors have helped me hone a particular skill. Other mentors have been guiding beacons in seasons of choppy ministry waters. Yet, I have to acknowledge that a deeper kind of growth happened as the direct result of relationships with those who have mentored me for spiritual development.

What is mentoring for spiritual development? Mentoring for spiritual development is the cultivation of both a real time discerned awareness of and active cooperation with the action(s) of the Holy Spirit through intentional and yielded spiritual interaction between seasoned ministry leaders and their emerging Kingdom counterparts.

WHAT DOES MENTORING FOR SPIRITUAL DEVELOPMENT LOOK LIKE?

Mentoring for spiritual development is a practice adaptable to a variety of contexts. As the regular rhythm of mentoring takes place (with the inherent conversations, prayer, reflection, Scripture, laughter, etc.), you can incorporate aspects of mentoring for spiritual development into the nooks and crannies of your mentoring relationship. However, a few components of mentoring for spiritual development are expressed in the disposition of the mentor.

- Maintain a posture of being resolutely "for" your mentees. This is not the same as agreeing with or affirming everything your mentees assert or want to try. This is having their back, standing with them when they fall or fail.
- Cultivate an active predisposition to seek and pray for the leading of the Holy Spirit together and to put into practice all that you discern to be from the Holy Spirit.
- Surrender your need to "be right" or appear to be the outcomes expert. Entrusting final outcomes to the work of the Holy Spirit will be a constant discipline for you to practice as a mentor.[2]
- Nurture a shared conviction that the Holy Spirit is active, engaged in the lives of Christ followers, and participating in ongoing communication with us.
- Practice the ability to be yielded to one another out of reverence for Christ.
- Be curious with the Holy Spirit about life, decisions, discipleship, and leadership.
- Adopt the role of advocate/guardian of a process rather than herald of a particular outcome.

CASE STUDIES IN MENTORING FOR SPIRITUAL DEVELOPMENT

Even with all of these postures in place, it may be challenging to imagine how mentoring for spiritual development happens in real time.

Case 1: Mentoring for Spiritual Development Using the Bible

I encourage reflective learning with your mentees, particularly through active reflection on scripture. This practice can be a fantastic life-giving catalyst for growth. However, as you have no doubt experienced the potential always is there that this activity may devolve into an exchange of interpretative differences and exegetical nuances. As a mentor you can assist in the spiritual formation of your mentees by steering them away from exegetical technicalities and toward spiritual development through a shared *lectio divina*-like practice.

As mentor, guard this process. It may be wise for you to start simply by connecting relationally with your mentees around questions of family, shared experiences, and so forth. Then, when it seems fitting, turn the conversation clearly to a spiritual focus by inviting your mentees to reflect on a biblical passage together. Be clear with them that this is primarily a listening exercise, not an exegetical one. You can then start by offering a prayer of surrender to all that the Holy Spirit desires to give you from the Word of God. Then proceed with the reading of a scripture passage that you have previously identified. Read this passage slowly, and out loud. Then, sit with your mentees in a time of devoted silence before the Holy Spirit and the biblical text. Discipline yourselves to be creatively attentive to the images, ideas, words, concepts that the Holy Spirit brings to your minds. After a few minutes of silence, invite your mentees to share what they experienced in the time of silence. Then, you can share what the Holy Spirit seemed to be saying to you. Resist the need to "be right" or nuance your shared reflections. Strive simply to place everything that is pertinent from your time of silence "on the table" for shared reflection.

You may feel the urge to stop at this point and draw some conclusions. At times this may be precisely the right action to take. However, you might be wise to resist this impulse. Instead, consider entering into a second time of prayer. Take turns with your mentees prayerfully presenting to God all you have already heard. As you do, actively ask the Holy Spirit to show you what, if anything, is particularly important. You could pray a simple prayer of, "Holy Spirit, help us discern what is vital and important for us to pay attention to so that we can hear clearly and only from you." Consider also reading the passage a second time.

Give yourself the freedom to repeat this prayerful process as often as is needed to feel settled about what God is saying to you both. This process is helpful because of its biblical rootedness, its insistence on quiet attentiveness to the Holy Spirit and a mutually experienced yieldedness before God, the Bible, and another human being. From experience you know that this practice can develop our capacity to hear and receive from God in community with others.

Case 2: Mentee Self-Reflection

You know that in critical moments in your relationship with your mentees, significant learning happens through Holy Spirit-led reflection on specific events in ministry and life. This can arise in a variety of ways: your mentees may present an issue for discussion, they could be wrestling with a decision, or possibly wondering aloud about a facet of ministry leadership. In these moments resist the urge to provide your expert advice. Instead, you could invite your mentees to participate with you in a yielded time of directed, listening prayer.

This time of listening prayer is similar to *lectio-divina* but without the deliberate use of a biblical text. You can begin with a clear invitation to the Holy Spirit to speak to, teach, convict, and so forth. You may find it helpful to declare aloud your faith-fueled desire to hear only from the Holy Spirit.

After an opening prayer of surrender, sit together in active spiritual silence. Remind your mentees to maintain an internal alertness to the words, images, emotions, people, biblical passages that the Holy Spirit brings to heart and mind. Take a minute or two to dwell together in silence. Then take turns sharing what you heard in the time of silence. This might seem like an awkward or strange practice at first. You may need to resist the internal urge to edit their sharing. Share courageously as an act of yieldedness to one another.

Once the sharing has taken place, ask questions such as: Is anything obvious to you? Are there discernible answers/learnings that you sense are from God? Do you have questions that flow out of the sharing? You may need to fight the impulse to reach any conclusions. Consider praying together again about all you have heard. Be curious with the Holy Spirit about all you have heard. You can repeat this cycle of prayer, listening, and sharing as needed. Even once you have arrived at what you believe to be a shared conviction born out of your listening prayer together, test it with scripture. Does your learning fit with biblical revelation? Is there resonance with what you know of God's character?

MENTORING FOR SPIRITUAL DEVELOPMENT WITH TEAMS

You can also pursue a version of mentoring for spiritual development on or with teams. It often results in a shared spiritual growth and development. As mentor to the group or team, you can use versions of the processes already presented to help teams make ministry decisions, grow spiritually, and develop a shared capacity to listen to the real-time work of the Holy Spirit.

Two benefits are clear. First, this process may help you and your mentees with decision making and discernment. After all, Jesus promised us that the Holy Spirit would teach us all things.[3] You will also discover that over time the regular practice of yielded, communal spiritual listening grows our capacity confidently to recognize the active voice of the Holy Spirit in our lives and ministry; the capacity confidently and communally to know the leading of the Holy Spirit is life giving for Christ followers of every age.

WHAT OBSTACLES MIGHT WE ENCOUNTER?

Your mentoring for spiritual development will encounter the same basic challenges that accompany all apprenticed learning. However, the unique nature of mentoring for spiritual development often will require that you address some specific challenges, including:

- *Private and/or Customized Faith*: We live in an age of privatized faith convictions and myopic faith formation. You will discover that this can make yielding to one another a challenge.
- *Public Yieldedness*: Most of us profess a yieldedness to God in private. However, publicly yielding our hearts will be a challenge for many of us. You can encourage each other with the biblical reminders about the inherent relational nature of the Christian faith. Spiritual development is a team sport.
- *Conviction or Guilt*: Your mentees may need help distinguishing between these two spiritual forces. The shame associated with guilt will cause many of us to gag on invitations to spiritual transparency. Conviction, however, is the territory of the Holy Spirit.
- *Perceptions of Relational Need/Trust*: Your mentees likely place a high premium on relational trust as a prerequisite for spiritual sharing. As a mentor, trust that relational depth grows when trust and spiritual mentoring are given freely as a starting point in a new relationship.

QUESTIONS TO AID THE PROCESS

Your work as a mentor will be aided by the courageous use of a few simple but powerful questions. Consider using variations of these questions regularly and liberally in your mentoring relationships.

What do you think Jesus would say about our conversation?

What do you think the Holy Spirit wants to clarify for us in this situation?

Would you join me in asking the Holy Spirit to speak to us about this decision? passage? challenge?

Would you pray with me about this?

A catechism in our tradition teaches this about the Holy Spirit.[4]

Q. What do you believe concerning "the Holy Spirit"?

A. First, that the Spirit, with the Father and the Son, is eternal God. Second, that the Spirit is given also to me, so that, through true faith, [the Spirit] makes me share in Christ and all his benefits, comforts me, and will remain with me forever.

The Spirit is indeed given to us. With joy let us discern and join the Spirit in ministry.

QUESTIONS FOR REFLECTION

1. What practices does your tradition encourage for "living in step with the Spirit of God"?
2. Recall a time when you vividly sensed the leading of the Spirit. What was that experience like?
3. How does it make you feel to be spiritually vulnerable with others?

SUGGESTED READINGS

Barton, Ruth Hailey. *Pursuing God's Will Together: A Discernment Practice for Leadership Groups*. Downers Grove, IL: IVP Books, 2012.
———. *Strengthening the Soul of Your Leadership: Seeking God in the Crucible of Ministry*. Downers Grove, IL: IVP Books, 2018.
Petersen, Eugene. *The Contemplative Pastor: Returning to the Art of Spiritual Direction*. Grand Rapids, MI: Eerdmans, 1993.
———. *Under the Unpredictable Plant: An Exploration in Vocational Holiness*. Grand Rapids, MI: Eerdmans, 1994.
Willard, Dallas. *Hearing God*. Downers Grove, IL: IVP Books, 2012.

Chapter Four

Mentoring for Healthy Boundary Making and Boundary Keeping

Jill Y. Crainshaw

> So as I live my life then, this is what I am trying to fulfill. It doesn't matter whether I become a doctor, lawyer, housewife. I'm secure because I hear the sound of the genuine in myself and having learned to listen to that, I can become quiet enough, still enough, to hear the sound of the genuine in you. [1]

Attending to voice. This, for me, is where healthy boundary making and boundary keeping begin for pastoral leaders. God calls us to speak with wisdom in the face of challenging life realities. God also calls us to listen with wisdom—and generous hospitality—as we embody pastoral tasks such as preaching, praying, baptizing, burying, and marrying. Out of these tasks (and others that are a part of ministerial work) and their link to Howard Thurman's emphasis on "the sound of the genuine" emerge several questions that motivate my healthy boundaries work. Perhaps you will find them useful as you embrace your call to mentoring:

- How do we as pastoral leaders face into all conversations but, in particular, into hard conversations with care and courage?
- How do we cultivate relational and reflective space that is safe enough for people to be brave in sharing their stories, fears, woundedness, hopes, and dreams?
- How do we discern appropriate boundaries—and appropriate life limits— out of which we can respond to these questions in life-giving and even community-transforming ways?

These questions are vital as pastoral leaders work to cultivate life-giving relationships with people in their communities. They are also questions central to religious leaders' efforts to support and mentor each other.

How do we support each other as we explore and embody healthy relationships? Three elements are essential for grounding this work.

MINISTRY AS A PECULIAR AND PARTICULAR CALLING

Religious leaders sometimes need to be reminded of the importance of healthy boundary making and boundary keeping. To be "set apart" for ministry is to be invited into people's lives and stories in ways that other professionals are not. We are authorized by our callings and our communities to baptize, bury, and marry. We also share meals, coffee conversations, and significant life moments with countless people in our ministering communities and beyond. Often, we are invited into the vulnerable places of people's lives because of our status as persons "set apart." This peculiar status means that we make decisions every day about where limits exist, not only in our ministries but also in our day-to-day activities. We also decide each day what boundaries we can and cannot, must and must not cross. Both boundary making and boundary trespassing (for example, when we report child abuse to local authorities or take a prophetic stand against unjust policies) are prophetic work and demand care in discernment and courage in embodiment.

The work of ministry is relationship-centered and can have ambiguous boundaries (including boundaries related to work hours, family ministry involvement, etc.). Also, ministry questions and concerns are becoming more complex with each generation of leaders (consider, as an example, the complexities of social media use and ministry today). This means that discerning healthy ministry practices is ongoing work. Although it may be hard to see when "healthy boundaries" denominational and/or presbytery requirements and workshops are announced, exploring healthy relational limits and renewing our commitment to making life-giving choices about how we use our time is a vital part of ministerial vocations. Discerning healthy limits is essential to maintaining a positive self-image as a leader. Living healthy life limits is vital to modeling the belief that we are created in the image of a God who respects and values who we are as individuals and who we are in community with others. Also, healthy and vital ministries rely on trust and mutual support to create spaces of welcome and safety for all.

LISTENING FOR THE SOUND OF OUR GENUINE

A second element central to the work of healthy boundary making and boundary keeping is captured by the phrase "the sound of the genuine." Theologian Howard Thurman emphasized in a 1980 baccalaureate address at Spelman College the centrality to his ministry and faith of listening for the "sound of the genuine" in himself and others:

> I must wait and listen for the sound of genuine in you. . . . For if I cannot hear it, then in my scheme of things, you are not even present. [2]

A primary reason why pastoral leaders find themselves in relationship quagmires or are undone by ethical complexities is because they have neither listened for nor attended to the sound of the genuine in themselves with adequate care. The most critical relationship ministers nurture is their relationship with the genuine—with God's image and spirit—within themselves. Thurman said our own life stories and woundedness can become the most recalcitrant challengers to our sense of well-being and worth. We also put at risk the well-being of others when we respond to pastoral dilemmas without adequate attention to our own brokenness. Thurman insisted that the only way we gain access to the sound of the genuine—to the sound of God—in ourselves is by meeting ourselves with God's love and being honest about our own scars, wounds, and shortcomings. Once we have done this, we are better equipped to listen for the sound of the genuine in others; in other words, to cultivate transformative relationships with people we meet along our vocational journeys.

As mentors, we have a sacred opportunity to share with our ministry colleagues and students incarnational conversations that birth God's Word anew in our midst. As mentors, you can invite ministers who are new to pastoral leadership to explore Thurman's concept of the sound of the genuine and encourage them to adopt spiritual practices that make them more aware of both their woundedness and their giftedness for ministry. You also have an opportunity through mentoring conversations to uncover together strategies for embodying theological ideals that are at the core of healthy communities and relationships.

TOGETHER THE BODY OF CHRIST;
INDIVIDUALLY MEMBERS OF IT

Ministry students and clergy who participate in my healthy boundaries workshops often are most concerned about and focused on instances of sexual misconduct and other violent or illegal activities, such as financial misappropriation, in their ministry settings. They want to know how to prevent misconduct and how to respond to it when it happens. This focus is understandable and important given the prevalence of clergy sexual misconduct and the realities of child sexual abuse in congregational and denominational life today. Religious leaders have a responsibility to be aware of the risks—both risks present in their own stories and risks within their ministering commu- nities—and to know what steps to take to respond. As mentors, you can share with those new to pastoral leadership what you have learned in your own ministries and through ongoing healthy boundaries work about the risks present in ministry today. You can help new religious leaders to be aware of denominational guidelines and community resources.

Often overlooked is the extent to which healthy responses to ethical di- lemmas in ministry emerge out of the leader's own self-awareness and theo- logical centeredness. Clergy sexual misconduct and other abuses of power too often are the result of *un*healthy boundary making that has occurred across a leader's life span or that has developed over time as the leader's personal life story becomes overwhelming or painful (due to marriage diffi- culties, job stress, conflict in the setting, personal health changes or crises, and/or other challenges). Religious leaders who are aware of their own vul- nerabilities are better equipped to respond in healthy ways to woundedness and its repercussions when they encounter both in their communities.

Lack of clarity about what constitutes healthy professional relationships can also emerge when pastoral leaders compartmentalize what is called the spiritual work of ministry (preaching, teaching, leading worship, praying) and what is viewed by many as the managerial or administrative tasks of faith community leadership. As a mentor, you have an opportunity to join new pastoral leaders in a process of defining or clarifying anew the primary theological values and principles that ground both their and your broad sense of calling or vocational identity and their and your daily ministry activities. Questions such as the following can invite shared dialogue about individual and communal values that shape a holistic perspective on ministry:

- What are our values as individuals and as communities of ministry? What is our compass (theological and/or spiritual) for living life together? How do our decisions about our life together—all of them, including those that seem mundane—help us to live out our values?
- What challenges to healthy relational dynamics do I as an individual and we as communities face?
- What relationship opportunities and risks do we anticipate as we seek to lead transformative spiritual communities?
- How do our decisions and actions as leaders and communities further our mission to incarnate a Christ-centered relational ethic and thus embody God's grace and love?

Each of these questions is related to boundary making and boundary keeping, work that religious leaders and their communities do explicitly and implicitly as they discern first, what it means to embody life together in the image of God; second, how they will relate to and care for one another in times of celebration and lament; and, third, how they will strengthen boundaries that support safe and peaceful communities. These questions also provide theological and spiritual grounding as leaders and communities discern what boundaries they will transgress for the sake of what they hear God calling them to be and do.

HOLDING SPACE AND HEARING GOD'S VOICE

Ministry is one of the most demanding professions we can be chosen and choose to embody. Why is it worth the effort, sacrifice, and risk? Pastoral leaders have unique opportunities to hold space so that people who are resisting or seeking or birthing something in their lives can be brave enough to respond to situations and circumstances out of their own insight and strength. For religious leaders, to hold space with and for others means to enter into vulnerable places with them and be with them without judgment and without attempting to control the outcome.

A biblical concept for holding space is "abiding" (see the Gospel of John). To abide with others means to join their journey as trustworthy and compassionate dialogue partners. To abide means to listen and empower another's voice. As mentors, when we abide or hold space with those we are mentoring about healthy boundary making, we invite them to give voice to their fears and woundedness around ethical issues in ministry. We adopt a stance of incarnational listening that, instead of giving advice, encourages and empowers our students and those we supervise to listen within themselves for how God is calling them to respond. Can you remember a time when a mentor listened with care for your voice in the midst of a noisy place in your life or ministry? What listening and mentoring strategies from that experience can you share as you hold space with other ministers who are struggling to hear God's voice in themselves or in a noisy and wordy world?

A comment from one of my healthy boundaries students reminds me of the importance of abiding with each other as we work to embody life together in the image of God:

> [W]e must face the fact that because people look to clergy for answers to many questions, there is an incredible amount of weight given to the opinions and advice of ministers. In my experience with seeking guidance regarding my call to ministry, my pastor's careful ability to listen without pushing his opinion on me was an appropriate use of power. It was a healthy use of authority and a positive experience that led to a great outcome.

As mentors, you have an opportunity to listen and ask powerful and empowering questions that model for new ministers a key element of healthy boundary making.

Shaping and sustaining healthy boundaries is at the heart of God's call to religious leaders to care for others. Healthy boundaries work also is essential to God's call to communities of ministries to advocate for justice and peace for all people. What surprises some people is the extent to which boundary work is vital to our callings to care for and protect the earth. We learn to hold all of the earth's space sacred—from cityscape jazz to mountaintop woodland melodies—when we have listened with spirit ears and God-tuned souls to the sound of the genuine in us and all around us. As we continue to grow in our own capacity to listen for the sound of the genuine in ourselves and others, we cultivate for each other and those we mentor places where their peculiar and particular voices can be heard and where they and we can discern God's voice anew for our times.

SUGGESTED READINGS

Blodgett, Barbara. *Lives Entrusted: An Ethic of Trust for Ministry*. Minneapolis, MN: Fortress, 2008.

Fluker, Walter. *Ethical Leadership: The Quest for Character, Civility and Community*. Minneapolis, MN: Fortress, 2009.

Lebacqz, Karen, and Joseph D. Driskill. *Ethics and Spiritual Care: A Guide for Pastors, Chaplains, and Spiritual Directors*. Nashville: Abingdon, 2000.

Chapter Five

Mentoring for Life-Giving Relationships

Isabel N. Docampo

> I remind my seminary interns that ministry is a marathon, not a sprint, and therefore requires long-term relational sustenance. Who are their friends in ministry? What is the structure by which they will gather these friends together to share the questions, the struggles, and the triumphs of ministry?

This is perhaps one of the most important conversations that this experienced supervising pastor has with his seminary intern during the internship. More important than this advice, however, is how well this supervising pastor models this wisdom. Students learn by what they see you do more so than what you say. When was the last time you gave yourself the space and time to gather with your friends in ministry? When was the last time you met with a spiritual director or professional counselor?

"Every pastor needs a therapist and every therapist needs a pastor"[1] is the excellent advice that a clinical psychologist offers at our annual orientation. Finding the right rhythms is important work because of the unrelenting pace of ministry. If not checked, it will overtake you.

> Stressful living is life in a state of prolonged, unhealed woundedness and unfed hunger. Obviously, we all have occasional times of stress, but this does not become stressful living unless we ignore the signs and warnings of our bodies and emotions.[2]

Seminary students preparing for ministry look to you, their supervisor-mentor, for guidance on how to integrate regular exercise, spiritual practices, and peer friendships of support into their everyday life. What will your students see you model?

Supervisor-mentors often thank us in the end-of-the-year evaluations for the supervising experience because it helped them to deepen two areas of their ministerial life. First, they report that it helped them sharpen their own theological reflection skills on their ministry practices; and, second, it challenged them to deepen their commitment to their own soul care and strengthened and/or affirmed the value of their peer networks. Not surprising, the interns in their final evaluation papers identify that their greatest growth occurred in these same two areas. One of my recent students wrote the following on the final self-reflection paper:

Soul-Care
During one of my mentor pastor sessions, he ended the conversation with "be good to yourself." It was that conversation and those words that gave me new vigor to in fact, "be good to myself." My goal is to keep a sustained focus on this competency, taking each day at time, as it will abet me in living my best life now.

Reflecting Theologically
I have learned what it means to take up the task of "faith in search of understanding" in the midst of a tremendous internship experience juxtaposed with life's diurnal demands. Essentially it forced me to deliberately discern God's activity in pedestrian, complex, and even tragic experiences. This exercise profoundly impacted my ability to reinvigorate a life-giving faith within.

THEOLOGY-IN-ACTION: THE COMMUNITY OF JESUS

Soul care through peer relationships is grounded in a theology of an intrinsically relational Divine Being at the heart of the Gospel. The Good News of Jesus is that the Divine desires creation and humanity to be in relationship with Godself and with one another characterized by an intimacy that heals limitations of fear, punitiveness, and sin. The Good News frees us to share generously mercy and justice with one another so that the poor are fed, the oppressed are freed, and the blind can see.

Jesus traveled with a community of friends bringing this Good News. These friends included the twelve known as "the disciples" as well as Susanna, Joanna, Mary, and Martha. These were Jesus's ministry friends with whom he shared many conversations, prayer vigils, and meals. Some had profound experiences with Jesus as when he took Peter, James, and John to the mountaintop and was transfigured before them with the accompanying voice, "This is my Son, the Beloved; listen to him!"[3] On the night of his arrest and death, Jesus was accompanied to the Mount of Olives by these same three beloved disciples. Following Jesus's horrific execution, in their shared grief, this larger circle of friends encountered the resurrected Jesus. As we know, this group went on to create the early Christian Church. He took his friends with him as he preached and healed the people. Soul care in and through healthy peer networks is how Jesus ministered. But Jesus also took his friends to the sea or the mountains for conversation, prayer, healing, and to simply rest. The poet Wendell Berry captures this in "The Peace of the Wild Things":

> When despair for the world grows in me
> and I wake in the night at the last sound
> in fear of what my life and my children's lives may be,
> I go and lie down where the wood drake
> rests in his beauty on the water, and the great heron feeds.
> I come into the peace of wild things
> who do not tax their lives with forethought
> of grief. I come into the presence of still water.
> and I feel above me the day-blind stars
> waiting with their light. For a time
> I rest in the grace of the world, and am free. [4]

LOVING YOURSELF/EMBRACING YOUR WOUNDS

> The mystery of ministry is that we have been chosen to make our own limited and very conditional love the gateway for the unlimited and unconditional love of God. Therefore, true ministry must be mutual. [5]

Henri Nouwen understood well the importance and challenge before you, the supervisor-mentor. The first step is to allow yourself to be caressed by the Divine and admit your woundedness, as Wuellner aptly outlines in her book *Prayer, Stress, and Our Inner Wounds*. She asks an important question: "Do we really believe that God does not infinitely care that we, friends, disciples, servants, are hurting and needing the healing touch?"[6] Healing is made possible when the Divine meets us as we reach out to one another in mutuality. You cannot heal yourself, although as part of a helping profession you often are tempted to try.

Henri Nouwen makes the case for the necessity of a community of mutuality so that collectively we can find the courage to follow Jesus into the homes, hospitals, city halls, streets, and homeless shelters with mercy and justice. He writes,

> I am convinced that priests and ministers, especially those who relate to many anguishing people, need a truly safe place for themselves. They need a place where they can share their deep pain and struggles with people who do not need them, but who can guide them ever deeper into the mystery of God's love. [7]

CULTURAL BARRIERS

Soul care through healthy peer networks is hard work because of the subtle hold of our culture's value of independence over us and our church members. Seminary students struggle with the pressure to be deemed fit for ordination by their denominations in a culture that extolls good leaders for "being available to all" and having "strong, top leadership." Even though the words "collaborative leadership" and "communities of practices" have been introduced into the church lexicon, the independent, strong leader model lurks underneath. These expectations weigh heavily upon you and seminarians. Introducing an interdependent, collaborative model of leadership is challenging because it is misunderstood as "weak." Our seminarians are met with resistance from without, surely, but most debilitating, *from their own self-talk*. That also may be true for you. For this reason, as a supervisor-mentor, you must take refuge and strength from your community of friends, just as Jesus took refuge and strength from the women and men of his close network.

For women clergy and seminarians, cultural expectations of leadership can be very confusing. Assertiveness often is termed aggressive or authoritarian ("She just gets so bossy," "She's a control freak"), and collaborative leadership as uncertain/unsure or worse, weak ("She just won't make a decision"). One longtime supervisor-mentor participates in a network of women clergy friends who meet monthly, and she makes a point of letting her interns know that this is sacred time in her calendar. She openly discusses issues of leadership with all of her interns, male and female, and the gender inequity that is implicit in how women clergy's leadership is perceived. She feels it is a benefit for both male and female seminarians to fully discuss gender inequities awaiting them in their future congregations because these limit everyone. Gender inequities create an ineffective binary construct of gender identity and gender-based gifts for ministry. Her invitation to discuss this is well-received by the seminarians hungering for this type of honest conversation. Her willingness to make herself vulnerable to them is mutually edifying. She models the type of mutuality that Nouwen described.

A SELF-CARE CHECKLIST FOR SUPERVISOR-MENTORS

As you prepare to supervise and mentor seminarians into the practice of ministry, it is helpful to take a self-inventory of your spiritual health as a Christian leader. Several resources can help you. Let's explore the contributions of Flora Slosson Wuellner and Henri Nouwen.

Wuellner suggests five areas for self-introspection. The first is "leadership fatigue" or the belief that it is all up to you, or super-responsibility that creates anxiety, annoyances over trifles, or apathy. Ask yourself: "Have I allowed others to look on me instead of God as the limitless fountain of loving activity?" "Do I feel that if I don't see to it, everything is going to collapse?"[8]

A second is an unawareness of inner wounds, hurts, or loneliness best discovered by a sense of numbness or lack of feeling inside for a long period of time. Observe your feelings throughout the day—when and with whom you are feeling "threatened, left out, conspicuous, at ease or relaxed."[9]

Third, the stress of feeling the "sensitive pain felt on behalf of others" that is shared by most clergy. Set aside intentional time of prayer to release the sensitive pain back to the Divine so that is does not debilitate your soul.[10]

Fourth, the stress of internalizing the problems of others that can be emotionally draining. The symptoms might be a sudden onset of irritability, anxiety, change in energy, or exhaustion that arise in certain groups, or with a particular person.[11]

Fifth, the pitfall of equating yourself with your work and to judge your self-worth only by results. She writes, "One of the greatest signs of spiritual growth is the emerging willingness to release results into the hands of God."[12]

Nouwen warns against three subtle temptations all clergy face—the temptations to be *relevant, popular,* and *powerful.* He writes:

> Jesus asks, "Do you love me?" Jesus sends us out to be shepherds . . . and be led to places where we would rather not go. He asks us to move from relevance to a life of prayer, from worries about popularity to communal and mutual ministry, and from leadership built on power to a leadership in which we critically discern where God is leading us and our people.[13]

The counsel of Wuellner and Nouwen could help structure the conversation of your clergy peer group so that you can move into deeper conversations and support for each other.

CONCLUDING REMARKS

Being a supervisor-mentor is a ministry to the church and to the world. As you share your faith and experience with someone who has felt a call to Christian vocation, trust that the Divine is walking alongside you, guiding and nudging you for mutual growth. Guiding your mentees to see how *you* lean into Divine grace to tend to *your soul* within a community of mutual friends is a profound gift that will shape their lives and those with whom they minister.

QUESTIONS FOR REFLECTION

A good place to begin is to ask yourself, "Are you being good to yourself?" just as the pastor exhorted my student. The wisdom I gathered from experienced supervisor-mentors is that preparing yourself before the seminarian arrives at your church is essential for a meaningful mentoring experience. They suggest that each new supervisor-mentor take the time to consider the following:

1. Consider how you embrace your interdependence with others.
2. Identify the theological and faith practices that help ground your ministry.
3. What type of soul care and healthy peer relationships do you have in place? If not, select a set of trustworthy, ministry friends to meet regularly for support.
4. Consider a monthly session with a spiritual director or a counselor, or both.
5. Do you have a friend, within or without the world of ministry, whom you may call at any time?
6. Do you plan an intentional day on a weekly basis for rest and renewal (not chores)?
7. Do you make time on your calendar for a longer time for renewal at least three times a year?
8. Do you have a regular exercise routine?
9. Do you have an interest outside of ministry, such as sports, the arts, or a hobby?
10. Complete a self-care assessment, such as this one: https://www.therapistaid.com/worksheets/self-care-assessment.pdf.[14]

SUGGESTED READINGS

Duke Clergy Health Initiative: Flourishing, https://divinity.duke.edu/sites/divinity.duke.edu/files/documents/chi/Flourishing%20Report.pdf.

Nouwen, Henri J. M. *In the Name of Jesus: Reflections of Christian Leadership.* New York: Crossroad, 1996.

Wuellner, Flora Slosson. *Prayer, Stress, and Our Inner Wounds.* Nashville: Upper Room, 1995.

Chapter Six

Mentoring for Pastoral Imagination

Eileen R. Campbell-Reed

"God is in this place."

That was Naomi's[1] first thought. She was a college senior. And at that moment she was standing in the midst of two thousand Mennonites singing in four-part harmony.

"This is who I am. This is the church. This is what I must do."

Naomi says her call to be a pastor "wasn't like a call from God as much as an expression of the community and expression of the faith and body of the community that said, *this is what I must be. This is what I must do.*"

The powerful moment of calling from her faith family set Naomi on a pilgrimage of preparation. Along the way she was mentored by professors and pastors, by situations, and by seminary assignments. Each gave shape to her growing pastoral imagination.

Theological field education (TFE) faculty and staff aim to create the conditions that will allow for positive mentoring toward a robust pastoral imagination. From my experience as a researcher and field education professor, I believe three areas of TFE are especially significant for transforming the ecology of teaching and learning such that it supports the long arc of learning the practice of ministry over time:

1. supportive mentors and supervisors who can make the right kind of learning space;
2. contracts and covenants that clarify the learning goals and expectations for a ministry placement; and
3. assignments, especially case studies, that formalize and seal in the learning of practical wisdom or pastoral imagination for students.

I hope to encourage your work of mentoring for pastoral imagination by taking you deeper into Naomi's story and considering the structural components of reflection, learning contracts, and case studies.

In the Learning Pastoral Imagination Project, Christian Scharen and I have had a front-row seat over the past ten years on how new ministers grow and develop their practice of ministry over time.[2] We have been following fifty pastors and ministers since they graduated from seminary. The purpose of the LPI study is to bear witness to how *pastoral imagination* forms and grows. The notion, first described by Craig Dykstra, is an embodied, relational, and integrative capacity for seeing the holy depths of a situation and knowing how to make a fitting pastoral response.[3]

This practical wisdom for ministry can only be cultivated over time and with experience. At the five-year mark of the study we noted, "Learning pastoral imagination requires both apprenticeship to a situation and mentors who offer relational wisdom through shared reflection and making sense of a situation."[4]

PROFESSORS, MENTORS, AND SUPERVISORS

Three years after Naomi's powerful moment of pastoral calling, she found herself sitting in the field education office of Viki Matson at Vanderbilt Divinity School. Naomi was two years into her seminary education and wondering how she would find a congregational internship. Professor Matson has deep knowledge about the kind of settings students need for flourishing, and she maintains a wide ecumenical network. The Mennonite world is relatively small, and having come out as lesbian in college, Naomi knew her options for service in a Mennonite congregation were limited. Naomi and her professor wrote letters to three congregations seeking a summer internship. One of those churches responded, and they began a phone interview process.

The urban Mennonite congregation makes decisions by consensus.[5] In a congregational meeting to decide about calling Naomi as their intern, a young person rose to speak, saying, "I can't imagine being called to ministry and not having a place to serve. And I hope when I get to where Naomi is, that there is a church that welcomes me in." Naomi says no one stood aside at that meeting.[6]

Summer came, and Naomi traveled to the urban ministry setting. On her first day Naomi was up early and ready for her orientation. Even before breakfast she was plunged into a ministry with people living on the streets. She recalls arriving at the church—a converted theater—at six in the morning. "It was just incredibly awkward for me. And I met the other volunteers from the church, and I didn't know what to say or do. And there was some food there for the homeless people and for us. And so we sat around tables together and one of the more experienced volunteers made casual conversation." Over the next two hours, Naomi took in a lot: scattered conversations with language that sounded inappropriate to her Mennonite ears. She noticed, "People were hung over, smelled like alcohol, went out to roll their cigarettes. No one in my family smokes! Some people traded tobacco with each other."

Naomi told us, "I come from a very pious family where I never saw alcohol except at my friend's house. So, here I was sitting at the same table with homeless people who had struggled with addiction and different kinds of management of their financial resources and their family resources. And one couple that comes in who had (I learned later) a pattern of abuse. She was bruised and had a black eye, perpetually, it seemed like. And it shattered my vision, for like, church, and what is church, and who is church. Completely gone! And after that—*the learning came after that*—as I processed that throughout the summer."

The lead pastor, Wayne, and two other members of the pastoral team at the urban church sat with Naomi at different times throughout the summer, and they listened carefully to "all the things that collided in that one morning." At one point, Naomi recalls sitting with the community ministry pastor, Becky, and "going on a half hour rant about systemic injustice." Rather than explain the problem away, Becky listened, and then she said, "Yeah, that's a tough question. There's no answer to that." She let Naomi own the complexity of the problem.

Thus, from Naomi's first moment of shattered vision, and by way of building relationships with the pastors and church members, including people struggling with homelessness and addiction, Naomi says her theology and practice of ministry changed in lasting ways that summer. For example, Naomi says that her "pristine idea of church community" and "baptism as the gateway to the Lord's Supper" all went out the window as she participated in a new kind of community. And the "pure ideals of worship" shaped by her rural Mennonite upbringing began shifting. She says, "To sit at a table with a homeless person and hear their story or see their struggle—*that* is worship, *that* is communion."

Clearly through Naomi's narratives, we see the ways her supervisor-mentors approached their work with a sense of pastoral presence and wisdom that is relational, embodied, and integrated. Pastors Wayne and Becky lead their urban Mennonite church to make practical judgments that lead to greater flourishing and love of neighbors, and it extends to their capacity for supervision and mentoring budding ministers such as Naomi.

MOMENTS OF MENTORING FOR PASTORAL IMAGINATION

When we observe what pastors Wayne and Becky did, we can see particular skills and perspectives that supervisor-mentors need for supporting students in their growth and flourishing toward a robust pastoral imagination. Naomi's story instantiates how her supervisor-mentors were able to make space for a learning trajectory that includes these moments:

• seeing the "more" of a situation;
• sorting through the possible responses and judging which action might be most fitting;
• responding by taking a risk and responsibility for one's actions;
• receiving feedback from mentors and others who are part of the situation;
• integrating the learning into one's identity and future attempts to lead pastorally.

Working with Professor Matson, Naomi received a lesson in seeing the situated possibility of finding a ministry setting given the constraints of her life and calling. Together they took a calculated risk by asking three churches to make space for Naomi to learn in practice. The church and pastors also took a risk on welcoming Naomi into their community, and they did it using a familiar decision-making process, which allowed them to hear the wisdom of the young as well as the seasoned members of their congregation.

Naomi experienced an immediate and enduring action-reflection process of learning ministry throughout her summer internship. With each overwhelming experience, the pastoral team accompanied her with conversational mentoring, reflecting on all that shattered her vision. They gave her space to think about and unpack the "more" of the situation in the neighborhood around the church. They also supported her in seeing the "more" of her own Mennonite tradition in conversation with a new-to-her situation of ministry on the ground.[7]

The pastors also struggled along with her "in the same boat" over how to reform the impulse in Mennonite worship to be orderly when that direction did not always make room for everyone in worship or around the communion table. By bringing Naomi into the pastoral team, they made opportunities for her to plan worship, preach, and attend regional meetings. In all of these practices of ministry, the church and pastoral team helped Naomi reconstruct new ways of seeing and thinking and leading.

On the final day of her internship, the church made space for Naomi to lead the service and to begin incorporating her newly forged understandings of worship and communion. She preached *about* the communion table and brought the words and reflections of a variety of people in the community into her sermon. At the center of the service stood a large communion table that Naomi described as "overflowing with fresh raspberries and blueberries. And the best strawberries you've ever tasted and local breads." The abundance of this final moment of the summer internship was also rich with Naomi's learning. It overflowed with the relationships she formed through the summer, and the communal support of church members, homeless people worshipping with the church, and her pastoral colleagues. Her shattered vision was recast by a summer full of immersion in the community.

To close the service, Naomi says, "They formed a circle around me and sent me off with blessings. And one of the junior high kids said, 'May other people be as nice to Naomi as she's been to us.'" And another older woman told her, "You belong in the church. May the church recognize that you belong in the Mennonite church." Both Naomi and the community of faith leaned into newly integrated ways of seeing and being the church that summer.

COVENANTS, CONTRACTS, AND CASE STUDIES

David Wood, an early adviser to the LPI Project, pushed us to think about this question: *What conditions are necessary for pastoral imagination to develop and grow?* In addition to mentors and supervisors, two more elements are important for creating the best conditions to cultivate pastoral imagination in students:

1. a covenant or contract that includes explicit learning goals and clear expectations, and
2. case studies that allow TFE students to take stock of their learning beyond the lived moments of ministry.

While meeting Vanderbilt's requirement for two years of field education experience, Naomi completed a learning contract with goals and expectations for each of her field education assignments. She wrote case studies that helped her integrate the learning from her experiences.

A clear and thoughtful learning covenant works best when students are able to discover and create the goals out of what they need to know to be more effective ministers. The seminary or divinity school with which you are a partner will provide a specific format. The contract establishes expectations and parameters for students, as well as roles and responsibilities for supervisor-mentors. Helpful contracts provide clarity and stability regarding hours, compensation, start and end dates, areas of responsibility, supervision meetings, and reporting. Whatever format these documents take, they should be more than paperwork or hoops to jump through. They should reflect the needs and expectations of both learners and the communities they serve.

The assignments for TFE courses are designed to foster integration of learning. Often case studies are written, presented, and discussed with peers, faculty, and supervisor-mentors. They are the kind of assignments that help make the learning stick over time. Case studies hold the possibility of formalizing TFE learning that may happen in multiple iterations in the ministry situation and during informal conversations. Case studies also allow students to go deeper yet, into the "more" of important ministry moments to make additional spiritual, pastoral, and theological connections, which recast their vision for ministry.

Naomi experienced solid mentoring toward pastoral imagination in her summer internship. She learned from her professor, her supervising pastors, the community of faith, and from her own formal and informal reflections. Because we have continued to follow Naomi as part of the cohort of fifty seminary graduates, we also have the profound experience of seeing how her integrated learning took shape over the next decade following that summer of "shattered vision." Just a year after seminary graduation, the same urban Mennonite church where she did her internship called Naomi as their interim pastor. When recounting the story of her call to be an interim, Naomi reminded us of her Mennonite roots: "That's where I'm called to be. *That is who I am.*"

Theological field education can both shatter one's vision for ministry and also recast new ways of seeing and being the church. Having wise mentors, meaningful learning goals, clear contracts, and formal case studies does not guarantee the cultivation of pastoral imagination. Yet each component does purposeful work in the discovery and learning process. And stories such as Naomi's show how important your role is for budding ministers to set them on a pathway for continuing to cultivate a robust and flexible pastoral imagination that serves faith communities and the wider world.

QUESTIONS FOR REFLECTION

1. How do you make space for students to come alongside you in ministry and "get into the same boat" with you and others to experience unsettling and powerful moments of ministry?
2. How do you help students to see the "more" of their ministry situation(s)?
3. What reflective learning tools (such as case studies) are in place to help your students integrate and formalize their ministry experiences?

SUGGESTED READINGS

Campbell-Reed, Eileen, and Christian Scharen. "Ministry as Spiritual Practice: How Pastors Learn to See and Respond to the 'More' of a Situation." *Journal of Religious Leadership* 12, no. 2 (2013).

Scharen, Christian. "Learning Ministry over Time: Embodying Practical Wisdom." In *For Life Abundant: Practical Theology, Theological Education, and Christian Ministry*, edited by Dorothy C. Bass and Craig Dykstra. Grand Rapids, MI: Eerdmans, 2008.

Scharen, Christian, and Eileen Campbell-Reed. *The Learning Pastoral Imagination Project: A Five-Year Report on How New Ministers Learn in Practice*. New York: Auburn Studies, no. 21 (Winter 2016).

Three Minute Ministry Mentor (3minuteministrymentor.org) video and podcast series with host Eileen Campbell-Reed.

Chapter Seven

Mentoring for Resilience

Susan L. LeFeber

Why do some students bounce back quickly after deep difficulties, whereas others give up or withdraw? *Resilience* is the ability to stay flexible, spring back, and recover after negative experiences, and you as a mentor can help to cultivate skills and abilities in those given into your charge. Some of the key areas for mentoring for resilience are

- fostering deeper self-awareness,
- building an understanding of systems, and
- nurturing lifelong habits of spiritual formation and self-care.

A closer look at each of these will help you consider application in your own context.

DEEP SELF-AWARENESS

One of the great privileges of working in field education is walking alongside students during God's amazing work of transformation as they move from bewildered novices to skilled and caring practitioners. In these few years they change and grow in many ways, and as a supervisor-mentor you have been given the responsibility of listening, loving, sharing, and co-shaping this formation.

Growing self-awareness often comes as a surprise to students as they begin their field education experiences: a first sermon or hospital visit can become a pivotal point of discovery. In the process, they uncover new God-given skills and gifts and learn that some tasks of ministry bring them immense joy but also realize that some duties prove to be more difficult than they ever imagined. You can watch, listen, and help them to pay attention as they work on one of the building blocks of self-awareness: *a well-defined understanding of one's skills, abilities, and strengths, as well as clarity and humility around one's weaknesses.*

But self-awareness also includes a *deeper knowledge of one's own core values and beliefs*, through developing theologically and the continuing discernment of God's call. Is there heartfelt restlessness for the marginalized and oppressed, or a sense of call to enter congregations in conflict? Are there passions from experiences before seminary in health care, teaching, or social work that shape values in ministry? Again, supervisor-mentors are privileged to be present for these moments of discovery, and you can help to probe and reflect, and give shape to these experiences.

Both of these forms of awareness, clarity around strengths and weaknesses, and deeper knowledge of core values and beliefs, contribute to changing *identity* in this amazing process of pastoral formation. It is an honor to be there when a student comes away from a hospital bedside and says, "Wow. I am a pastor!" But it's even more important to help students reflect on the experience in light of their larger identity and articulate more specifically (and authentically), "I am a pastor who . . ." Being able to fully inhabit this awareness greatly contributes to resilience. Authentic identity creates a solid foundation based on clear thinking and deep truths that will help students to withstand difficulties and emerge stronger.

As a supervisor-mentor you can also create challenges and train for healthy responses, for instance, in coaching to receive constructive feedback. With a strong authentic identity in place, a resilient student will be able to hear criticism with humility and a desire to improve. If the response is anxious or defensive, you have an opportunity to shape expectations and build these skills.

One of our most experienced supervisor-mentors (more than thirty students so far) says that the messages she repeats most often come under the heading "Know thyself":

> Know your strengths and weaknesses and when you are most susceptible to making errors in judgment, and return to your core values and beliefs when faced with temptation. Be authentic to your true self, the one that God has called and continues to shape. [1]

And one of the joys of my own work is reading the student reflections on how they are growing, both in their skills and goals, and in their formation as disciples in faith. I take great care in pondering and discerning with them: "This is what I see: you are developing in your thirst for justice in your community. Your prayer practices are shaping the way you listen to others in your Bible study. God is at work here . . ." God is at work in our mentoring relationships as we help to bring clarity and strengthen awareness that in turn strengthens resilience.

THE SYSTEMS AT WORK

We all live in *complex webs of relationships*, and students' webs are especially layered. Home, family, church, job, classmates, faculty, friends, God, and internship all compete for time and attention. The skills in self-awareness discussed above may need to be repeated in other spheres ("What are my strengths, weaknesses, and core values as a parent, a student, an employee, or a friend?"). Any one of these spheres can be a source of challenge or difficulty that requires skills in resilience.

A poor grade on a midterm, a child rushed to the hospital, a toxic work environment, or a fight with a friend all will affect the student's performance (and much more) in the context of your mentoring relationship. You have rich opportunities to model health and resilience in your own webs of relationships and to share wisdom on how to navigate these trials in positive ways.

At the same time, it is important for students to understand that every other person inhabits the same webs of relationships, and that in a congregation or field context, *tangles of power and anxiety* have existed long before they arrived. Other chapters in this book talk much more about leadership and contextual awareness, but for now it's important to remember that respect for and understanding of the systems and all of the multiple forces at work contribute to resilience, that flexibility in the face of challenge. Just as students' own self-knowledge is at the core of resilience, an awareness of the systems at work in their context will help them to manage expectations and develop clarity about their own role in the system.

While these skills help students to grow in wisdom about when and how to act appropriately, they also help them to understand when situations are out of their control. Recently, a very talented student in my care was assigned by her denomination to a small struggling congregation. She preached the gospel, taught Bible studies, and led a training course for lay leaders. She saw glimpses of hope and vision for the future. But when the congregation experienced a series of deeply stressful and uncontrollable events, their old patterns of anxiety and dysfunction returned, and the decision was made to close the church.

"What did I do wrong?" she asked me. "What could I have done better?" We talked about all of the systems that were at work long before she got there and how her role as student pastor fit into their story. We recalled her strengths in school, her loving family, and all of the support from her colleagues and mentors in the denomination. We examined the processes at work, affirmed her identity, abilities, and values, and managed expectations. In her final reflection on the experience, she wrote of the joy of preaching the love of Christ and the bright spots she had seen along the way, and the tremendous growth in wisdom she had gained from the privilege of being allowed, as a mere student, to walk with a congregation in its last days.

This perspective on the systems at work brought about great growth in resilience for her. As a supervisor-mentor, you can build resilience not only by passing along your skills in leadership and conflict resolution, but also by helping those in your care to read the patterns, understand their place in the story, and stay true to their authentic selves.

SPIRITUAL FORMATION AND SELF-CARE

In the *Flourishing in Ministry* Project, Matt Bloom and colleagues have done extensive research into the kinds of self-care that are most effective in promoting clergy well-being and preventing burnout. They divide them into three categories: recovery experiences, restorative niches, and spiritual disciplines. [2]

Recovery experiences are times when the individual can detach completely from tasks and responsibilities. These may be experienced daily for short periods of time (for instance, a walk at lunch), or in the practice of Sabbath. Their research showed a longer time of several days away provided optimal results in more and better resilience. [3]

A *restorative niche* is time spent in a creative activity in which an individual has some expertise, one that fulfills a passion and brings joy in accomplishment: for instance, gardening or painting. My own restorative niches are knitting and baking (I am an expert, I am passionate about the materials and techniques, and the products are satisfying). More than a simple hobby, a restorative niche encourages deep immersion into a state of joy and truly "restores" flexibility and positive balance. As a mentor, you have the responsibility to model these practices and encourage your students to take the time they need to rest, as well as to engage in a creative pursuit for deeper restoration.

But *spiritual connection* is the key to all resilience, and is far more important than any factors listed above. Among our own students and alumni, there is a direct correlation between those who are most resilient and those who are able to articulate with certainty that God is at the center of all life, all work, all ministry, and all love.

One of our recent excellent students has lived with a lifelong disability and has faced many roadblocks and obstacles along the way. He has overcome each with great humor and perseverance, but sometimes he admits to being very tired and discouraged. In his final semester of seminary, he was blessed with an insightful supervisor-mentor, who asked him, "Are you a rowboat, or a sailboat?" This supervisor-mentor helped him to raise his sails and changed his life.

Like congregations, seminaries are filled with people facing persecution, personal tragedies, conflict in their families or workplaces, and difficult diagnoses. The students who also make space for God and look forward each day to deepening that relationship bounce back again and again. This is not a simple formula, but rather a deep understanding that self-awareness and identity are created by and lodged in the person of Christ. Our web of relationships is held together at the center by Christ, and the time away and activities that give us joy are provided for us through the gifts of Sabbath rest. The foundation of time and space with God will not be shaken. May God bless you as you share your wisdom and open space for God's amazing growth in this holy work.

QUESTIONS FOR REFLECTION

1. How did you arrive at clarity about your own core values and authentic identity? How can you share this journey with your students?
2. Think of the web-of-relationship spheres in your own life: how do you hold these together in balance and harmony? What wisdom can you pass along to your students?
3. How do you detach and find restoration? What are your own best spiritual habits? We learn prayer best from others. How will you pass this along?

SUGGESTED READINGS

Burns, Bob, Tasha D. Chapman, and Donald C. Guthrie. *Resilient Ministry: What Pastors Told Us about Surviving and Thriving*. Downers Grove, IL: IVP Books, 2013.

Funk, Mary Margaret. *Thoughts Matter*. Collegeville, MN: Liturgical Press, 2013.

Peterson, Eugene H. *Under the Unpredictable Plant: An Exploration in Vocational Holiness*. Grand Rapids, MI: Eerdmans, 1992.

Steinke, Peter. *Congregational Leadership in Anxious Times: Being Calm and Courageous No Matter What*. Lanham, MD: Rowman & Littlefield, 2014.

University of Notre Dame. "Flourishing in Ministry: Emerging Research Insights on the Well-Being of Pastors," 2013, https://workwellresearch.com/media/images/Emerging%20Insights.pdf.

Chapter Eight

Mentoring for Theological Reflection

Matthew Floding

Making sense of experiences you've had in ministry, grounding them in the good news of God in Christ, probably mark the most meaningful that you have had. You can appreciate in hindsight the pivot points, marked by grace, in which deep formation took place in your life and in others. Experiences such as these come to mind:

- profound encounters at the Table or Font
- weathering challenges and discovering resources for resilience
- the wonder of God speaking into congregants' lives through preaching
- mysterious encounters with seekers
- encounters with God in prayer
- birth and death
- moments of collective courage to act

MENTORS MODEL

As an experienced pastor you've worked at mastering this capacity to do theological reflection; or maybe better, being mastered by it. Share your experience. Share the language of scripture and theology come alive in imaginative meaning making of ministry events. Like the pastor who told me about a congregational vote to plant a new church, "Forty years ago the congregation voted against planting a new church; to play it safe, not risk the unknown. They marched right up to the Jordan, turned away and then wandered in the wilderness. This time they have discerned God's call, are trusting God's provision, and we're crossing over."

Your student is willing to cross over and be open to joyful, terrifying, and vulnerable experiences. They will need your help to reflect meaningfully on them. As you embark on this internship adventure, risk mutuality with this colleague-in-formation. As Brené Brown has taught us, "The result of this mutually respectful vulnerability [will be] increased connection, trust, and engagement."[1]

CULTIVATING ATTENTIVENESS

Because this is a new context for your student, cultivating attentiveness is important. This, too, is mentoring for meaningful theological reflection. A reflection exercise such as the Ignatian *Examen*, practiced by them at the end of each day, will encourage this.[2] It counsels a review of the day following this pattern:

• Become aware of God's presence.
• Review the day with gratitude.
• Pay attention to your emotions.
• Choose one feature of the day and pray from it.
• Look toward tomorrow and pray toward it.

Engaging in a practice such as this will help your student discern what they might bring to your weekly reflection conversation. I appreciate that it focuses on God's presence and gratitude. It's a healthy reminder that God already is at work in your ministry context. This, in turn, will encourage inhabiting ministry as spiritual practice and nurture reflective practice.

A CORE CONVERSATION: CALL

Invite your student to share their call story with you. Make space for them to share it on several occasions and with diverse groups—for example, with the leadership team/council, at a youth group gathering, with a senior's Sunday School class, in a children's message, as part of a devotional during a mission team's service. Encourage each group to ask questions. Your student will actively construct their ministerial identity as they form and share the story in various contexts.

Sometime later, you can provide the sacred space for them to pause, ponder, and reflect appreciatively on what they experienced sharing their story with the various audiences. Questions such as these can serve as prompts for further reflection.

• What are you hearing reflected back to you?
• Where are there points of continuity and what new insights are emerging as you tell your story?

- What biblical stories or persons do you find helping you understand your own story?
- Are you experiencing a heightened sense of energy for particular theological or missional themes as you share your story?
- Has sharing your call story grounded you further in your tradition? In what ways?
- Where do you sense God active in this unfolding narrative?

Mentoring your student for theological reflection means continuing to explore the contours of their call through the variety of ministry experiences they have.

AUTHENTICITY, INTEGRITY, AND FAITHFULNESS

Your student longs to cultivate their own capacity for theological reflection. How else, they wonder, can I minister with authenticity? This is the cry for receiving the gift of identity formation through what you and your congregation or ministerial setting reflects back to them. It revolves around personal questions. "I believe I am called to ministry. Do the people of God discern this too? What all is God summoning out of me for ministry? Who am I? I feel I need to be more self-aware. How do all of the particularities of my life such as gender, race, sexual orientation, abilities, and age fit into my call? Am I socially aware, so that I can recognize and honor these particularities in others for the sake of authentic ministry?" Whether right out of college or an adult-in-transition, all begin again, novice, who needs to grow into their authentic ministerial identity.

How else, they wonder, can I minister with integrity? This is the cry for experiencing the disparate and disconnected fragments of theological, biblical, and historical information they have received in the classroom coming together to inform embodied ministerial practice. They, too, have an acute awareness that their life is fragmented. Experiencing integration happens as all of these fragments connect with core themes that emerge in their life as ministry is practiced. "Where do I see God gathering up the fragments into a more integrated whole?" It is quite literally their story connecting with God's story for the good of the world.[3]

How else, they wonder, can I minister with faithfulness? This is the cry for keeping faith with the Church catholic, capital "T" tradition, while inhabiting a small "t" tradition. It is deeply wondering about how I inhabit faithfully this tradition with all of my particularities. It is the anxious question, "How do I intersect with the Tradition, my tradition, and with others who inhabit a different tradition so that my interaction and collaboration with them participates joyfully and fruitfully in the Kin-dom over which Jesus reigns?"[4] This is closely related to the cry to engage with proper confidence in interfaith dialogue and shared ministries for the common good.

Each of these cries is a curriculum for theological reflection.

Unlike the classroom, the primary text for theological reflection in field education is your student's experience as they practice ministry.[5] Each experience in ministry opens wide the possibility of reflecting with your student on questions of authenticity, integrity, and faithfulness. This kind of reflection coupled with the possibility of engaging that ministerial art again can foster growth toward competency. It can also nurture pastoral imagination, that "distinctive and very special kind of intelligence that enables them to engage in pastoral work of real creativity and integrity, and to sustain it over many years."[6]

THEOLOGICAL REFLECTION IN ACTION

When they bring their experience to the reflection time, you can encourage a flow to the reflection:

- Describe the experience.
- Engage in analysis.
- Weigh carefully responsible ministerial engagement and discern potential invitations to future ministerial action.

It's something like the inductive Bible study questions, What? So What? and Now What? or Catholic social teaching's See, Judge, Act, or methodical engagement using the Wesleyan Quadrilateral's Scripture, Tradition, Reason, and Experience. You can weave into this movement questions that explore authenticity, integrity, and faithfulness.

If their ministry experience is the textbook (in all its complexity including perceived effectiveness, feelings, social analysis, images that come to mind, and more), its conversation partner is the Tradition/tradition (including scripture, theology, history, and liturgy). This correlation is at the heart of theological reflection.

In your reflection times the balance of the conversation may be tilted toward one or the other. For example, your student preaches their first sermon in your context (or any context). Recall your own. Later that week the reflection conversation may lean heavily toward experience: nerves, delivery, time, illustrations, and so forth. After listening empathetically and reassuringly, you might gently invite reflection from the Tradition/tradition: "Have you ever wondered about the relationship between our words, the word, and the Word?" If you discern it to be appropriate, you might share your first sermon experience.

On the other hand, you may have a student for whom the Great Thanksgiving and the language around the sacrament of the Table is a new experience. Assisting you at the Table has raised all kinds of theological questions for them. You recall your first time presiding at the Table. Your reflection time later that week definitely tilts toward the Tradition/tradition. They press you with wonderings: sacrament, ordinance, or just a Christian practice? Altar, Table: are the two ideas compatible? How is Christ present? Why are the kids participating? You might begin by returning to their experience. "Let's explore those, but tell me, what did you observe and experience serving Communion? How did Christ meet you?" Then turn toward their specific questions. If you discern it to be appropriate, you might share an experience you have had while presiding at the Table.

Conversations such as these will surface opportunities to explore embedded versus deliberative theology. Their embedded theology are beliefs and commitments assimilated from family and faith community and assumed. Take the question of who takes Communion. Experiencing children participating in Communion provides the opportunity to interrogate their embedded theology or assumptions. Their deliberative theology, "the understanding of faith that emerges from a process of carefully reflecting upon embedded theological convictions," can emerge from your reflection time,[7] and finally, and this is not to be rushed, determine a faithful ministerial response or discern an invitation to future ministerial practice.

Here's one practical way to mentor theological reflection that will take some anxiety out of the conversation. Before your regular meeting, invite your student to create a two-column reflection report.[8] The first column simply reports the event. The second provides space to draw connections from scripture, theology, liturgy, describe feelings, and ask questions. Here's an example.

Report:	Reflection:
Jeremiah is a first grader with special needs. He has Greig's Syndrome. Claire, his normal Sunday School buddy, was going to be absent so we had asked a church member, Madeline, to fill in. We had barely begun our first game when Madeline gathered Jeremiah up and took him out of the room. She assumed that sitting and listening to storytelling would be too difficult for him.	* How does God regard human difference? * "Let the children come to me and do not prevent them. To these belongs the Kingdom" (Matt. 19:14). * "For it was you who formed my inward parts; you knit me together . . . I am fearfully and wonderfully made . . ." (Psalm 139:13f). * How might we have better equipped Madeline for this ministry opportunity? * We make the same promises at baptism to every child without regard to ability—to nurture faith, to model faith, to walk in faith together. We need to keep faith with Jeremiah.

These are our basic tools: the students' ministry experience, listening attentively with empathy, questions that encourage exploration, and—with discretion—our own formational story.

PRACTICE WITH THE REFLECTION BOX

What if they get stuck? They can describe the experience but don't know where to go next. I find this Reflection Box tool helpful. Consider the experience and start with what comes to mind first. Take reflecting on a hospital visit. Maybe it's how you felt. "I felt anxious entering a hospital room to visit someone who is suffering." You might turn next to what you did or evaluate how you performed. "I was glad to take my cues from the lay leader who knew the person. I think our prayer time brought comfort." Then explore what of the Tradition/tradition comes to mind. "God was there, the Good Shepherd accompanies us into the dark valleys of life—and death." Maybe it's awe or wonder, like Jacob declaring at Bethel, "Surely, God is in this place." And God is at work.

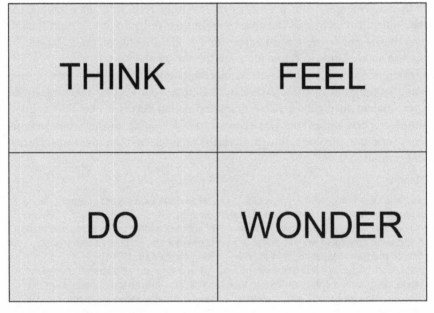

Figure 8.1. Reflection Box

The following are brief portions of real student experiences.[9] As you read them, in which box do you find yourself beginning? Walk through the remaining boxes in any order, naming what comes to mind as you practice this reflection method.

Overwhelmed

It was a dreadful and awe-full experience. I went to the hospital to visit the Petersons and their son Luke. I knew that he had been hospitalized for nearly a year, his whole life really. But, when I arrived at his NICU room, the nurse told me that his heart had stopped working. I entered and could only be a silent presence. Eventually, they held Luke in their arms, and I wrapped my arms around them and I cried as I prayed over them. Everyone seemed overwhelmed with grief.

But then suddenly this situation became a holy moment. When the family learned of the opportunity to take professional photos of their son for safekeeping, they invited this option without hesitation. The parents bathed their son's body and groomed his thick head of hair. I was witnessing a holy demonstration of love. As the couple took photos with their son in front of a white drape, these three people—mother, father, and son—whom I watched go through the painful shadow of death, suddenly seemed transformed. They were glowing! Ironically, they were all full of life.

Conflicted

I am the only white person who works on our team, which has felt like a special gift to me. The team has been unbelievably welcoming to me. Grace asked me if I wanted to start leading the devotionals at the upcoming workshops. As I have thought more about it, I really don't want to lead them, and frankly, I don't think I should. Most of the participants we work with are people of color. Grace, who typically leads these devotionals, is a woman of color and has been through this program herself. She speaks about God in a way that is authentic and clearly makes the participants feel comfortable and excited about what is to come next. It would be dishonest for me to try to replicate that.

The seminary field education program will offer your student training in theological reflection. You could use these scenarios with your student to reinforce the training, to try out the Reflection Box, and to discuss how complex and layered each ministry event can be. So much can be gained through the discipline of this mutually beneficial practice. Best of all, God will meet you there and empower you both for authentic ministry practiced with integrity that is faithful.

QUESTIONS FOR REFLECTION

1. Tell a story of how God integrated your seminary experiences and your ministerial identity in the first years of ministry using this image of Kintsugi pottery.

2. When has reflecting on a ministry experience resulted in a change of practice?
3. What works for you to practice theological reflection on ministry with colleagues?

Figure 8.2.   Kintsugi Pottery. *Source*: **Wikimedia Commons.**

SUGGESTED READINGS

Blodgett, Barbara, and Matthew Floding. *Brimming with God: Reflecting Theologically on Cases in Ministry.* Eugene, OR: Wipf and Stock, 2015.

Click, Emily. "Ministerial Reflection" and Charlene Jin Lee, "The Art of Supervision and Formation." In *Welcome to Theological Field Education*, edited by Matthew Floding. Herndon, VA: Alban, 2011.

Floding, Matthew. "Engaging in Theological Reflection." In *Engage: A Theological Field Education Toolkit.* Lanham, MD: Rowman & Littlefield, 2017.

Ji-Sun Kim, Grace, and Susan M. Shaw. *Intersectional Theology: An Introductory Guide.* Minneapolis, MN: Fortress, 2018.

Stone, Howard W., and James O. Duke. *How to Think Theologically*, 3rd ed. Minneapolis, MN: Fortress Press, 2013.

Chapter Nine

Mentoring for Cultural Humility

Ismael Ruiz-Millán

ENCOUNTERS

Our lives are about encounters. Our spirit first encounters God, our creator, even before conception. When we are conceived, we encounter our mother's womb. Once we are born, we encounter the world—and the encounters do not stop. Throughout our life span, we experience a series of encounters, with different spaces, places, and more significantly, we have different encounters with different people. These encounters, whether or not we like it, whether or not we notice them, shape who we are and, consequently, our ministerial practice and approach to theological field education.

When you add the ingredient of culture into these encounters, the complexity augments, but so do the possibilities of becoming an improved version of ourselves and enhancing our ministerial practice and approach to theological field education. The truth is that very often we make the dangerous assumption that because one of the foundations of our faith is "Love your neighbor as yourself," we are actually living it out. Therefore, when it comes to interacting with other cultures, we tend to assume that we automatically are seeing, appreciating, embracing, and learning from them.

As supervisors and mentors in field education, we cannot afford to ignore the power that culture has in the formation of how we view ourselves, others, and God, and how these views shape the way we engage with students in field education—especially students who come from cultures or backgrounds different from our own.

As a reflection group leader, and in my work with pastors in supervising and mentoring roles, I often find myself asking them to share about a positive or challenging encounter they have had with people from other cultures. They often share a story that would portray a "kumbaya" kind of moment, where differences did not matter and they were able to find common ground and universal values with the other culture. From time to time, I also have brave souls who share how anxious they feel and how stressful it is to interact with someone from a different culture, ethnic background, or race.

AWARENESS

As supervisor-mentors, we need to be aware of this tension and acknowledge it. In fact, naming this reality becomes an opportunity to model a healthy way to respond to the tension caused by our interactions with other cultures— especially challenging interactions. Especially when supervisors and mentors come from a privileged background and feel the tension when interacting with these students, they need to remember that the tension they might feel at that moment is what students from minoritized groups experience on an ongoing basis. Although it is important to acknowledge our own tension and anxiety, one also needs to have a good balance to avoid making it only about our own experience and feelings, diminishing and disregarding what the student from another culture is experiencing.

On the other hand, for supervisor-mentors from minoritized groups, we need to consider that we might be the first person in our role whom students from dominant cultures or from privileged backgrounds have encountered, which creates tension within the student and us. A part of our role should be helping students realize that they need to take responsibility for their own growth in interacting with cultures different from their own; they need to do their own homework. For instance, what I often hear from students or leaders from minoritized groups is that the dominant culture expects them to teach them how to establish and sustain relationships with minoritized cultures, which is another way to leave the heavy lifting to the minoritized group. As supervisor-mentors from minoritized groups, we need to offer support and guidance to students from dominant backgrounds. At the same time, we need to hold them accountable and help them shift their expectation that supervisors, mentors, and students from minoritized groups need to teach them cultural competency—this should be a responsibility for all.

CULTURAL COMPETENCY

The late 1990s marked the beginning of a movement within the human services professions that stressed the importance of *cultural competency*.[1] Psychology and social work were the pioneers; these fields emphasized cultural competency as a critical part of forming professionals for the changing realities of a new century. The idea of cultural competency came out of efforts to find alternative language to another term that was circulating: *cul-*

tural sensitivity. Miguel Gallardo notes that the main critique of sensitivity language was that it was more abstract and did not provide "a skill component."[2] With such a strong emphasis on developing concrete skills to enhance cultural competency for recipients of cultural competency tools and training, it also created the false notion that recipients were becoming "experts in culture" that ended up becoming stumbling blocks instead of cultural bridges because of stereotyping, arrogant gestures, and unwillingness to continue growing in cultural understanding. Supervisor-mentors should take advantage of the learnings from other fields to approach cultural competency by not seeing it as the end point, which becomes the source for more tension in cross-cultural interactions.

Stereotyping, arrogant gestures, and unwillingness to grow can sabotage a theological field education experience. For that reason, as supervisors and mentors in field education, we have the opportunity now to approach cultural competency from a different perspective and with a new language. Melanie Tervalon and Jann Murray Garcia introduced an alternative to cultural competency—cultural humility.

THE JOURNEY TOWARD CULTURAL HUMILITY

The premise of cultural humility is described in the following statement by Melanie Tervalon and Jann Murray-Garcia in their article "Cultural Humility Versus Cultural Competence": "Cultural humility incorporates a lifelong commitment to self-evaluation and critique, to redressing the power imbalances in the physician-patient dynamic, and to developing mutually beneficial and non-paternalistic partnerships with communities on behalf of individuals and defined populations."[3] In this article, they also highlight the principle of institutional accountability, especially institutions that perpetuate oppression and discrimination of minoritized groups.

As you supervise and mentor students, internalizing the cultural humility principles can help you to model what it means to be on the journey toward cultural humility. For instance, Paul noticed that the Romans were becoming arrogant, and he not only became aware of it, but he acknowledged the behavior to them and challenged them, "I say to everyone among you not to think of yourself more highly than you ought to think" (Romans 12:3 NRSV).

In the context of theological field education, and in our work as supervisor-mentors, the principles of cultural humility can be very helpful because they lead us to start the journey with no one else but ourselves. We start by adopting a posture of ongoing learning and critical self-examination and reflection. Very often, you might not be aware of the way you internalize biases, prejudices, stereotypes, and racist gestures. Adopting a posture of ongoing learning, but especially of critical self-examination and reflection, can lead us to discover areas in our lives that need redemption in terms of how we see, perceive, and relate to other cultures.

Recognizing and challenging power imbalances for respectful partnerships is another cultural humility principle.[4] The MeToo movement uncovered the many ways in which influence and power have been abused, including in ecclesial and ministry settings. Being open and honest in the way we use our power and influence in our interactions with students, especially students from different cultures, can make a difference in the kind of space we create for theological reflection.

Cultural humility principles in the context of ministry encourage us to find ways to develop and establish relationships in which we exercise what I call extravagant mutuality. Paul put it this way: "Do nothing from selfish ambition or conceit, but in humility regard others as better than yourselves" (Philippians 2:3 NRSV). Extravagant mutuality encourages us to go the extra mile in all of our interactions with other cultures. We then consider the other as better than ourselves, not to humiliate ourselves or perpetuate the idea of cultural arrogance, but rather we seek to emphasize the imago Dei in the other. Put differently, when we acknowledge the imago Dei in the other, we can now see the other as a contributor to our own lives (our view of God, others, and ourselves). This is especially important when we belong to the dominant culture or come from privileged backgrounds. What does it mean for us to consider others better than ourselves? What can we learn from our students if we would consider them better than ourselves, not just recipients of our experience and wisdom? How can we lead our students to ask what they could learn from their placements if they consider the people they serve as better than themselves?

Institutional accountability is another cultural humility principle. Often, field education has to respond to the larger policies of the institution. As supervisor-mentors, we should become advocates to create an optimal learning environment, even if that means challenging the institutions in which we serve.

The difference in challenging institutions while having the cultural humility principles as a reference is that we do it in a more authentic way because we do our own inner work first, then we analyze the way we use the power we hold, and eventually we transition to challenge institutions. The truth is that often, we try to challenge institutions without starting with ourselves first. The cultural humility principles lead us to model the change we want to see in others and in dysfunctional institutions.

As supervisor-mentors on the journey toward cultural humility, we will need cultural competency tools. However, in order to redeem these tools and to align them with the cultural humility concept, we need to see them as means of grace. Next, I share a story of how using cultural competency tools with an emphasis on grace, and with a connection to the concept and principles of cultural humility, can help us be better in our service as mentors and supervisors, and in leading others toward cultural humility.

REV. MITCH SELLER'S STORY

Rev. Mitch Seller[5] approached me a few years ago expressing his interest in being a participant in one of the programs I facilitate. Rev. Seller holds a senior leadership position in which he supervises and mentors hundreds of pastors, so his concern was whether he could participate in the program given the power and influence he held. My response had the first principle of cultural humility in mind (lifelong learning and critical self-reflection) by asking him a question. I invited him to be open to learn and experience something new, but I also challenged him to start the process of critical self-reflection. My question was simple: "How comfortable are you with being uncomfortable?"

Rev. Seller now shares how this question led him to challenge himself to be in a space where he would have to let go of his power and influence to become a fellow participant in the program. Later, as part of the program, he used a cultural competency tool, the intercultural development inventory (IDI),[6] which includes a one-on-one reflection session on the individual IDI profile. During our one-on-one session, in which I emphasized the importance of "regarding others better than ourselves," he expressed how realizing that he considered himself more culturally competent than he really was, along with the idea of what it would mean to really consider "the other" better than himself, was leading him to deeper reflection.

In other words, his critical self-reflection led him organically to move to the second principle of cultural humility (challenging power imbalances), which took the form of him realizing how uncomfortable he was going to be in a position of letting go of his power and influence in order to become an equal in the program. In addition, in relation to his supervisory and mentoring role, he now is more careful in using his power and influence. He now reflects on how this exercise of letting go of power and control for the sake of equality and equity has enriched his leadership.

Rev. Seller did not stop in the second principle, as part of his experience in the program. He also realized that institutional awareness was needed, which is a reflection of the third cultural humility principle (institutional accountability). He was able to secure funding for a three-year immersion program, in which key leaders would be exposed to the same principles Rev. Seller was exposed to. Rev. Seller is an example of how the cultural humility principles can work in a very organic yet powerful way.

As a last example, here is a note Rev. Seller gave to a team of ten key denominational leaders reflecting how he was letting go of his own power and influence to let me lead with confidence, but at the same time he was inviting others to do the same (institutional accountability):

> One final suggestion (and I mean this as gently as possible) . . . we are all leaders and used to being in charge. Let's allow Ismael to lead and make decisions. He is a gifted, kind, gentle and humble leader but he is a strong leader. In the midst of travel it's often not helpful to have 10 people telling you what you should be doing. He'll get us there and back . . . promise! Thanks!

Gestures such as this make a huge difference when we interact with other cultures and people different from us. They are especially important when we are trying to hold institutions accountable and challenging them to let go of power and influence so that people from minoritized or marginalized communities have opportunities to lead with confidence.

QUESTIONS FOR REFLECTION

1. As you think about your internal process and the way you respond to interactions with other cultures (especially challenging interactions) or people different from you, are there any areas in your life that need repentance or renewal?
2. Can you identify ways in which you hold power or influence over another person or group? How do you think others perceive how you use this power or influence?
3. In what ways are you challenging your institution when identifying systems or policies that limit transformation in your work as supervisor-mentor and in theological field education at large?

SUGGESTED READINGS

Adams, Maurianne. *Readings for Diversity and Social Justice*. New York: Routledge, 2013.
David, Eric John Ramos, and Annie O. Derthick. *The Psychology of Oppression*. New York: Springer, 2018.
Gallardo, Miguel E. *Developing Cultural Humility: Embracing Race, Privilege and Power*. Los Angeles: Sage, 2014.
McGuire, Kenneth, Eduardo C. Fernández, and Anne Hansen. *Culture-Sensitive Ministry: Helpful Strategies for Pastoral Ministers*. Mahwah, NJ: Paulist, 2010.
Sue, Derald Wing. *Multicultural Social Work Practice*. Hoboken, NJ: Wiley, 2006.

II

Mentoring for Ministry in Context

Chapter Ten

Mentoring for Leading in Systems

Nathan E. Kirkpatrick

In the tenth chapter of St. Matthew's gospel, Jesus sends His twelve disciples out to engage in ministry on their own for the first time. He offers some instructions for how they are to travel, what they are to do, and then concludes with this: "be wise as serpents and innocent as doves" (10:16 NRSV). It's a strange benediction for a first mission trip, and, yet, it is not a bad admonition for congregational leaders—be wise *and* be innocent.

As you mentor newer leaders in their work of navigating congregational and other institutional systems, part of what you are aiding them to do is to cultivate the capacity to be both. You are offering them a different vision of leadership than what they may have seen before—those dangerous experiences of ineffective leadership, leadership marked by the innocence of a copperhead or the cunning of a turtledove. Instead, what you are helping newer leaders learn is that it is possible and necessary to be both savvy *and* holy, strategic *and* ethical, political *and* pastoral. To lead effectively and faithfully in congregational and institutional systems requires the *and*. Through your mentoring relationship, you will model this before your mentees through your own ministry and you will help them come to embody this in their own.

Yet when we think about learning to lead congregational systems, how do we mentor toward the *and*? It may be difficult even to imagine the place to start. After all, we have an incredible body of knowledge and writing about the structures, dynamics, challenges, and opportunities in systems generally and in congregations specifically.

What are the necessary first learnings about leading in systems that support vibrant, vital future faithful ministry? I want to suggest three conversations to have with new leaders that can help them find their bearings and learn to inhabit the *and*.

First, newer leaders need mentors to help them explore what systems exist to do. Systems exist primarily to preserve what they care about most. As such, they are inherently conservative structures—not in the political sense but in the sense of safeguarding or sustaining something that is understood to be valuable, perhaps even precious. Denominations were created not just from disagreements or disputes but out of deeply held convictions that some theological truths are too important to lose, and without the structure of the denomination, they would be lost. Seminaries were born out of a conviction that an educated clergy in a particular geography or within a particular tradition mattered for the formation of generations to come of faithful people. Congregations were born as a way of carrying out the mission of God, however that was understood, within a particular community or within a particular family at a particular time. Something was too important to lose, and so systems were created to preserve it.

To preserve what they care about most, systems develop an internal culture with all of its trappings—symbols, stories, artifacts, language even— around the thing that is most valued. It is this culture that makes "us" who we are. In healthy systems, this culture serves not only to reinforce identity but to sustain vitality over time: "we are the church that hosts the city's soup kitchen," "we are the seminary that prepares students to embody a progressive gospel in the world," "we are the denomination that offers an unashamed Christian witness in a changing world." In dysfunctional systems, however, this culture often holds organizations captive with dramatic and ossifying effects: "we were the church that had eight hundred people coming to worship on Sunday mornings," "we were the flagship seminary of our denomination," "we were the embodiment of Christianity within American life and culture." Even in dysfunctional systems, a system's culture reinforces its identity—just not in ways that are conducive for a generative future.

These systemic cultures have another apparent and significant effect. They set expectations for leaders and members, defining "rewards" and "punishments" for compliance and deviation from organizational norms. In many cases, these expectations are unspoken but still palpable. Pierre Bourdieu, the French sociologist and philosopher, says that, over time, people learn to have a "feel for the game" that is necessary to navigate a system or culture. For newer leaders, that can sound a bit abstract, but it is important for them to understand that systems behave this way.

Perhaps an example will help to illustrate this. A few years ago, I worked with the clergy leaders of a sizable congregation in a major American city. In one of our conversations, the associate pastor told how, upon his hiring, he had been told by multiple people in the congregation that he should only wear a certain name brand of suit. "It's what we do here," he had been told. It may sound ridiculous, but in that congregation, what mattered most was image—both internally (how the congregation saw their clergy as professional and sophisticated people) and externally (how the congregation wanted to be viewed by those outside its walls). Systems create cultures, which create expectations, all in service of the thing that they care about most.

Having a conversation with your mentees in which you help them name how the systems of which they are a part work toward self-preservation and describe the culture of these systems is a first and necessary step in helping them lead in an "*and*" way. It is helping them to get their bearings on the ground.

One thing that may surface in such a conversation: your mentees may have observed that what actually matters most to systems with which they are familiar may be different than what that system states publicly matters most. For example, some congregations say publicly that what matters most to them is to be welcoming and inclusive, but in practice, the system cares most about familial bonds or preserving its homogeneity. Giving voice to this disparity and others like it is important because it can cause a kind of cognitive dissonance in the system that is not only worth the leader's noting but also worth the leader's time in challenging and changing.

Second, newer leaders need their mentor's help in understanding how people participate in systems. In order to lead in both wise *and* innocent ways, our mentees must be able to discern the differences between position and authority, role and influence. One mistake that newer leaders often make: they assume that within a system, position and role equate to authority, influence, and power. Sometimes that is true, but, often, it is not.

In the congregation I first served as a pastor, a woman—we'll call her Frances—made most of the decisions. She was not named to any of the church's committees and had not been for almost twenty years. If you asked her to serve on one, she would say no. Yet no decision was made in that congregation that, in one way or another, she did not approve. In that same congregation, one man—we'll call him David—served on every committee and was the first to speak about every issue. Through a series of weaker pastoral leaders, he had appointed himself de facto leader of that congregation. He was fiery and forceful in personality. Yet, David often was on the losing side of discussions in committees and on the opposing side of new initiatives and proposals. David considered himself the leader of that congregation and had many titles that would confirm that self-understanding, but no one in the sanctuary was following where he was leading.

Franceses are part of every system, in every organization and institution. They often have no formal position or role, and yet, they wield considerable authority and influence over everything the organization achieves. Most every system has Davids, too—people who have formal titles and enjoy positions of "power," yet they have little influence over what actually happens within the system.

Helping your mentees distinguish between role and authority is critical for their leadership. Here, you can help them cultivate a real curiosity about their system to prevent them from believing that the organizational chart accurately reflects how their system works. I would suggest that you have them engage in an exercise I learned in that first congregation when a congregational consultant came to help us with a visioning process. The consultant asked the members of the congregation to imagine that they had a difficult personal decision to make, and then, on index cards, write the names of the three people in the congregation they would want to talk to about that decision. They were to put their names on the top of the cards but were told that their answers were confidential, and they dropped them in the Sunday offering plate. As I reviewed those cards, what emerged was a fascinating map of authority and influence in the congregational system. Frances's name appeared on card after card; David's was on virtually none.

Having your mentees engage in a similar exercise may help them understand systems in a new way. As in my case, they may understand why the nod of the patriarch or matriarch moves mountains while the booming voice of the lay leader accomplishes little. They may be surprised at the hidden influencers and leaders within their systems and may find a new political savvy in engaging their congregation. (If surveying the whole congregation or institution would be impractical, your mentees could survey only the largest adult Sunday School classes or fellowship groups and create a similar map.)

In the third conversation, I would suggest that you invite your mentees to reflect on how they participate individually in the system they are leading. The aim of this conversation is a practiced self-awareness. Here, the questions you ask as a mentor are of paramount importance: How are you being both savvy *and* holy? Strategic *and* pastoral? When in ministry have you been too calculating? When have you been naive? When have you found yourself triangulated—cast into the role of victim or villain or vindicator? When have you avoided confrontation or conflict that needed to happen because you wanted to maintain the status quo? When have you done something because you wanted to be liked? What did you learn about yourself in these moments? These are the kinds of questions that this third conversation holds.

Each of these questions, in its own way, points to that larger and more important question about our lives as leaders—am I doing the internal work that is necessary for me to lead faithfully and well in this system? As leaders, it is when we say yes to this question that we lead with integrity in systems. It is then that we are leading from the place of "*and*." By asking your mentees to reflect on these questions (and by reflecting on them for yourself in the presence of your mentees), you are inviting the kind of self-awareness that helps ministry leaders thrive.

Of course, it is also when we are doing this kind of internal soul work that we can help systems to change. Sometimes when the topic of systems is broached, it can sound as if we are all helpless victims of their immutable machinations, but systems can be transformed. When we discern that systemic change is necessary, it is our integrity as leaders that allows us to facilitate that change because integrity is the seedbed of trust. From that place of integrity, we can call upon our relationships with congregants and other leaders to move a congregation forward—without using those relationships or those people toward our own ends. When they see us leading from that place of integrity, our people can trust that we will say what needs to be said and do what needs to be done, that we will invest ourselves even in the most difficult face-to-face conversations for the sake of the congregation's future.

"Be wise as serpents and innocent as doves," Jesus invites. Like all of the arts of ministry, perfecting the capacity to be both wise and innocent is a lifetime commitment. The conversations proposed here between mentors and mentees are merely the beginning of that work. Yet, I am persuaded that, accompanied by wise mentors asking good questions, our mentees can learn to lead faithfully and well in complex systems. I am also persuaded that they can do the sometimes-necessary hard work of transforming systems to be more faithful embodiments of the Kingdom of God on earth.

In the end, that embodied witness is why it matters that we learn to be both wise and innocent.

SUGGESTED READINGS

Friedman, Edwin H. *Generation to Generation: Family Process in Church and Synagogue.* New York: Guilford, 1985.
———. *Friedman's Fables.* New York: Guilford, 1990.
Steinke, Peter L. *Healthy Congregations: A Systems Approach.* Herndon, VA: Alban Institute, 2006.
———. *How Your Church Family Works: Understanding Congregations as Emotional Systems.* Herndon, VA: Alban Institute, 2006.

Chapter Eleven

Mentoring for Relational Conflict

Jennie Lee Salas and Margrethe Floding Jasker

Do you recall taking a course in seminary on relational conflict and learning models of conflict resolution? I don't. Yet, I do recall taking a course that taught me how to use scripture in addressing issues, especially relational conflicts that are experienced in the life of our faith communities.

Wasn't it at the Garden of Eden that the first relational conflict arose? God asked who ate the fruit. Adam blamed Eve, Eve blamed the snake, and Adam pretty much blamed God because God was the one who gave him the woman (Genesis 3:8–13). Does this sound familiar in your church or place of work, or even in your own family dynamics?

Yet, there is hope, and it is found in the gospel of Jesus Christ. God's word provides ways to respond to conflict, and God's common grace gifts in the social sciences provide insights to help us understand ourselves and others when conflict happens.

Do you recall the first time you were confronted with conflict in ministry? What was your initial reaction? A competitive urge to "win"? Avoidance, hoping that it would go away? Did you wonder how God was going to get you out of this situation?

BE TRANSPARENT

Don't shield your students. Allowing them to either witness or hear your stories of how you encountered and navigated such conflict can be informational and formational. The bottom line: conflict is inevitable.

I recall a recent incident in a theological reflection group that I co-facilitate. We had invited a guest who provides seminars on the topic of "Cultural Competency and Sensitivity." Some of the group members had conflicting thoughts and accusations. It was clear that the students in the group were hurt and angry. The following week as we gathered, we invited the group to process the experience through a theological lens. It was clear that the trust that had been established with the group for the past twenty-five weeks had been shaken up. However, what I witnessed was the trust that had developed at work. The group still honored the relationships that had been developed and the sacred space that we had established. I recall one student saying, "We don't learn how to deal with conflict in seminary." Your mentoring role in teaching and modeling how to deal with relational conflict is very important.

No one likes confrontation and conflict in ministry. It is stressful. It is personal. Further, conflict usually has been portrayed as a negative experience. It's one of the reasons that many of us shy away from dealing with conflict instead of seeing conflict for what it is: an opportunity to grow personally, in relationship with others, and theologically.

Knowing how you respond to conflict is the first step in being able to resolve it. Resolving conflict begins with you. You should know your own triggers, so that when you find yourself in a conflict—and you will—you can understand why. Conflict is normal. Emotions are normal, and they are your body's first defense if something is wrong or "off." You are not a failure because you find yourself in a conflict.

A professor in my master's program said to us, "Where is the peace that you are trying to find?" As conflict resolvers we have to know where we find our peace, which requires work and time. We need to be able to reflect upon our own reactions and feelings and ask questions such as: Where do those come from? Why did I react so strongly to that? Why did that one comment bug me more than all of the others? What do I value in myself and others? How are those values different from others' values? How do I react when I *think* other people do not see those values in me?

I wasn't diagnosed with ADD until my late twenties. I got through school by learning to read context clues and pretending not to care. After I was diagnosed and got on the right medication, I realized that I was kind of a type "A" person. I did care, a lot, and I finally had the focus and energy to care. To this day, a big trigger of mine is my perception that someone thinks that I am flaky, ditzy, or lazy—labels that can be wrongly applied to persons with ADD.

As a patient relations specialist it has been important to know and understand that trigger as I interact with patients, especially because I actively deal with the conflicts and triggers of persons who might lash out at me or project onto me because they themselves are scared or worried. Though it is uncomfortable, it's important to get to know yours, then know where to go when they go off. Ask yourself, "Where can I find that peace that I want to maintain?" Even harder, sit long enough with those fears or past experiences so that you can know them. As my professor told me, "You don't have to like them, but you should know them." Your students need to understand their emotional formation. The resulting self-awareness will serve them well in ministry.

UNDERSTAND THE DYNAMICS

Because I came to seminary after years of experience in the corporate and human services environment, I had faced various relational conflicts. At first, my initial response to conflict was to avoid it, or try to be accommodating because I was so uncomfortable with confronting the conflict. How do you react when encountering a conflict situation?

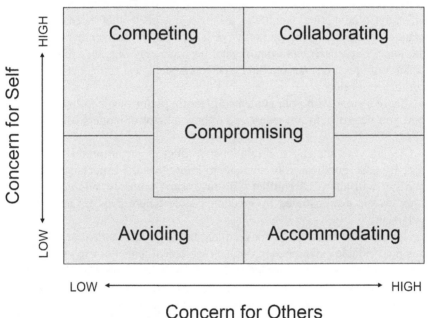

Figure 11.1.   Five Styles of Conflict

This diagram represents the five styles of conflict.[1] Every person has a conflict style. What is yours? Do you see conflict as a competition and want to win? Do you avoid conflict like the plague? Are you accommodating by giving up your "side" for the sake of peace? Do you try to compromise by finding a middle ground? Or, do you collaborate with the person you are in conflict with to try to meet both persons' needs? Conflict styles naturally change depending on who you are in conflict with (a conflict with a spouse will look very different than a conflict with a boss). It's good to know your go-to conflict style and the styles of those you are working with. For example, if you are a competitive type and your student is an avoider, it helps to know that so that you can enter into a conversation graciously, instead of feeling like the other person is running away.

No conflict style is bad. At times it is important to compete, for instance, when safety is involved. Collaborating gets the reputation as the ideal, but again, you need to weigh what is at stake before collaborating. You wouldn't collaborate with a two-year-old about whether he can run out in front of cars. That's just a no go.

A helpful story to understand the power of collaboration is one about two chefs fighting over an orange. They both said they needed the orange to bake their cakes. A competitor would want to "win" the orange, a compromise would be to cut the orange in half. An avoider would never engage the conversation, and an accommodation would be to let the other chef take the orange. Collaborating would be asking what each chef needs from the orange. When asked, one chef only needs the peel, while the other only needs the juice. Each chef gets exactly what he wants. By digging a little deeper and asking questions surrounding a person's needs, we can get creative with conflict resolution.

Share a story with your students of learning your own conflict style, and how you've grown in self-awareness of how it helps or hinders when conflict arises.

Assure your students that relational conflict is uncomfortable for everyone. It's also good for your students to know that the expectation is that a minister will approach conflict with love, care, empathy, and compassion. This love is demonstrated by meeting people where they are and without judgment.

Initiate conversations about conflict and invite the students to approach this unavoidable experience through a theological lens. For example, review and discuss a case study on relational conflict. Describe what happened, what was felt, what styles of conflict were engaged, and how God was present in the experience. These are reflective questions that can lead to formative conversations. The exciting thing is that mentoring seminarians in this important experience in ministry is an opportunity for mutual learning and a deepening collegial relationship.

The principles that are foundational to any approach to conflict underscore the value of the counsel that James offers: "be quick to listen, slow to speak and slow to anger" (James 1:19). I would add a fourth principle in the beginning and at the end: prayer. Prayer brings us back to God, centers us, and encourages us to seek God's wisdom and grace for these important relational encounters.

QUICK TO LISTEN

Listening is a basic practice in ministry. As we provide pastoral care, we listen more than talk. When faced with a conflict in the community of faith, being an attentive presence creates a sacred space that demonstrates care and concern. Deliberate avoidance of confrontation can lead to major dysfunction.

This is a time in our culture that is filled with so many distractions. Even for well-intentioned students, listening well can be a challenge. It isn't that they do not want to listen patiently; the challenge is that our society has conditioned this generation always to be on and never really off.

Listening is a learned art. It needs to be practiced. Perhaps your own listening skills have been impacted by receiving spiritual direction or participating in CPE. You can impact your students deeply by inviting them to bring a ministry report or something like a verbatim to your reflection time.

SLOW TO SPEAK

Miscommunication surely can be a culprit in conflict and disagreements. Your students can grow by observing your behavior while you patiently exegete the conflict. Share your thinking process with your students. The need here is not to try to fix the situation but to help the individual(s) go deeper into what really is going on for them. What may be that unmet need that has ignited a conflict? Asking clarifying and probing questions can result in a more adequate understanding of the conflict's roots.

Confronting conflict can be uncomfortable. Perhaps by changing the word to "carefrontation," your students will feel less intimidated or uncomfortable. David Augsburg coined the phrase "carefronting" and applied it to helping persons retain relationships, owning anger, inviting change, giving trust, ending blame, letting go of prejudices, and making peace. Learning to listen for understanding and speaking from genuine care can diffuse conflicts. Ephesians 4:15 reminds us that "speaking the truth in love, we will grow to become in every respect the mature body of him who is the head, that is Christ."

SLOW TO ANGER

Donald Capps wrote about the method of reframing. It is used by therapists, but he has found value in using this method while providing pastoral care. It invites the minister to take initiative in assisting the person(s) shift from a negative mode of expression to a positive one. Reframing is "changing words that can change the world." Have you ever seen the commercial of a blind man begging on the street with a sign that says, "I'm blind, please help"? A passerby sees the sign and notices that people are not really responding to it. She takes the sign and writes it differently, "It's a beautiful day and I can't see it." People who passed began to drop money in his cup. The point is that words can be helpful in obtaining a helpful perspective. However, words are powerful and when said with anger, can be destructive to the heart and spirit. James reminds us that anger can lead us to do things that can be wrong and hurtful (James 1:20).

Our final advice is that you make these two commitments to your student. First, practice. Conflict is not easy, it does not feel great, nor does it naturally make us want to engage. Practicing empathy, using communication styles that do not come naturally to us, and getting in touch with our feelings are challenging. The only way they can feel better about their own skill set is to practice. A great way to do this is to practice tough conversations. Role play with your students conversations about conflicts that you have seen in your congregation or conflicts that you are worried about that might come up. It will feel awkward, and honestly, you will be bad at it at first. But the more you practice, the more comfortable you will get, and the more you will grow your—and their—skills.

Second, be OK with being wrong. When engaging in conflict, it is very easy to become defensive. Challenge yourself to tear down those defensive walls that we want to build as soon as we feel we are being criticized. It also is OK to be wrong when you are the one trying to "fix" a conflict. If you are trying out your empathy tools and guess that a person feels like she is not appreciated, but it was really something else, that's OK! The fact that you are engaging and putting effort into hearing someone's pain can feel like a balm in itself. She will tell you if you are off the mark. The point is not to be right; the point is to be present.

Finally, prayer is what invites God into the circle of relational conflict. It reminds us in the beginning that we are loved and cared for, and at the end, it leads us in the path of righteousness, peace, and, at times, reconciliation.

QUESTIONS FOR REFLECTION

1. What is your conflict style?
2. What have you learned from relational conflict in ministry?
3. What biblical passage(s) informs your approach to relational conflict?

SUGGESTED READINGS AND RESOURCES

Brené Brown on Empathy, https://www.youtube.com/watch?v=1Evwgu369Jw.
Fisher, Roger, and Daniel Shapiro. *Beyond Reason: Using Emotions as You Negotiate*. New York: Penguin, 2006.

Furlong, Gary T. *The Conflict Resolution Toolbox: Models and Maps for Analyzing, Diagnosing, and Resolving Conflict.* Mississauga, Ontario, Canada: John Wiley and Sons, 2005.
Lyon, K. Brynholf, and Dan P. Moseley. *How to Lead in Church Conflict: Healing Ungrieved Loss.* Nashville: Abingdon, 2012.
Stabile, Suzanne. *The Path between Us: An Enneagram Journey to Healthy Relationships.* Downers Grove, IL: InterVarsity, 2018.

Chapter Twelve

Mentoring with Gender in Mindbodyspirit

Trudy Stringer

> I have more questions than answers, more problems than solutions, and of
> these gifts I freely give.

My late colleague Rev. Dr. Dale Andrews began each class with this quote,
and it is in this spirit that I invite us to consider the often fraught, sometimes
uncomfortable, and profoundly important subject of gender, our claims regarding theological anthropology, and their consequences.

I invite us to consider what *embodied* questions regarding gender our
students bring to the ministry of mentoring. Students' backgrounds, our own
histories, and students' learning contexts vary and will nuance these encounters. Using necessarily broad strokes, I invite you to consider with me implications for mentoring while engaging inherited stories, our students' stories,[1]
sacred texts, religious traditions, and theological claims in light of current
theological and public dialogue regarding constructions of gender.

GENDER AS A CULTURAL CONSTRUCT

How would you define *gender?* To help clarify my own thinking, I turned to
the American Psychological Association definition:

> Gender refers to the attitudes, feelings, and behaviors that a given culture
> associates with a person's biological sex. Behavior that is compatible with
> cultural expectations is referred to as gender-normative; behaviors that are
> viewed as incompatible with these expectations constitute gender nonconfor-
> mity.[2]

85

In other words, we are participants in our particular culture, and we define and redefine what constitutes gender and gender-appropriate behaviors, including sexual behaviors.

To complicate already complex issues, consider current research on our susceptibility to unaware prejudice. A Harvard social psychologist, Professor Mahzarim Banaji, among others, studies biases inherited from the cultures that we inhabit—and that inhabit us. The premise of implicit/unconscious bias is simple and humbling. We are formed and our worldviews are shaped in these cultures. This cultural conditioning goes far beyond our cognitive/ rational capacities to accept and reject ways of seeing the world, other human beings, and even ourselves in prejudicial ways.[3] From a Christian theological perspective,[4] we might use the language of systemic sin for this cultural conditioning that "others." We live in an era of contestation in inherited notions of what it means to be embodied, sexual, gendered human beings, notions we find reified in translations and interpretations of sacred texts and inherited religious traditions, assumptions, and sexual ethics. How do we as mentors of emerging faith leaders engage these complex and uncomfortable conversations?

A course on sex education in faith communities coincided with a student's internship in a congregation's summer camp addressing gender and sexuality. The student, seeking to engage "thorny topics" and "advocate for queer identities" in faith communities, found insight at this intersection of theology and practice, not only equipping the student with "language and foundation," but also inspiring the student to explore "the intersection between . . . sacred and sexual."[5]

What resources do we have to consider the intersections of sacred and sexual? How might we be complicit in sinful systems? Perhaps some of the texts in this chapter may offer insights.

"FEARFULLY AND WONDERFULLY MADE": GENDER BINARY AND GENDER FLUIDITY

> The ambivalence with which Christian thought focuses on the sex of the matter may be traced to a persistent somatophobia or fear of flesh.[6]

What does it mean to be "fearfully and wonderfully made" (Psalm 139:14)? The theological claim made in this ancient text reverberates in challenges some of our students bring to long-held religious traditions and assumptions. These students come to us embodying being human beyond the gender binary of male and female and its cultural dictates. They come to us struggling with inherited traditions that question whether they *are* made in the image of God. Other students come to us struggling with challenges to deeply held religious beliefs regarding gender and sexuality, challenges embodied in classmates, family members, and friends.

How does it *feel* to live in a body deemed unacceptable? One student intern reflected:

> I have . . . come to learn that experiencing homophobia and transphobia in my own life, in my own home, has led me to be afraid of myself. Not only this, but also set me on a ceaseless pursuit to save my parents, and those like them, from continuing to be afraid of people like me.[7]

What guides us as religious supervisors and educators when we encounter the embodied pain of religiously grounded rejection?

BODIES, FLESH, AND SIN

> But flesh has ambiguous connotations. Indeed, its materiality often carries the weight of sin.[8]

Because I am part of the Christian tradition, I focus here on its sacred texts, which evidence a conflicted relationship with bodies and flesh and invite each of us to reconsider messages in our sacred texts. On one hand we find the writer of the Gospel of John boldly proclaiming that "the Word became *flesh* and dwelt among us" (John 1:14 NRSV, italics mine); on the other hand, we engage biblical passages often interpreted to mean that our bodies, our flesh, somehow operate as the site of sin, a claim often associated with our sexuality and separate from our spirit (see Romans 8:5, 7–8 and Galatians 5:19–21). What are we to make of these competing claims? How do these claims influence our and our students' attitudes toward gender definitions, our bodies, and sexuality? How might we consider bodies, flesh, and sexuality theologically as good gifts? Perhaps it is to risk entering "the intersection of the sacred and sexual" and, as the student below suggests, "be attentive to our whole selves."

Engaging a course, "Sexuality: Ethics, Theology, and Pastoral Practice," deepened this student's theology and

> taught me the importance of the entire embodied self . . . revealed . . . the ways . . . I experience sexual shame in my mind and throughout my whole body because of the way sex was taught to me. It taught me that if our whole selves are called into something, we must be attentive to our whole selves.[9]

What might it mean to live in our "entire embodied self"? How might this way of living transform our practicing theology?

PATRIARCHY: AT WHAT COST? THE ME TOO MOVEMENT, THE VATICAN SUMMIT ON SEXUAL ABUSE, AND TOXIC MASCULINITIES

Cultural gender norms, sexual abuse, and violence have burst into national and international news cycles. The Vatican faces charges of deep complicity in decades of sexual abuse by its clergy; women's voices volubly narrate experience after experience of sexual abuse; men, especially the younger generation, question toxic masculinities, cultural constructions of maleness requiring repressed emotions while connecting virility with violence.

Patriarchy is an ancient, culturally constructed system that assigns binary gender roles that align with positions of more (male) and less (female) power, enforces these roles, and resists gender fluidity. Patriarchy has many faces particular to cultural contexts, while maintaining an anthropological stance of the heteronormative male of the species as dominant, a dominance exerted in what some critics define as toxic masculinities.[10] The current public dialogue calls us to question the costs of systemic patriarchy for victims, bystanders, *and perpetrators* entangled in the cycles of sexualized violence. How are we as theological educators and mentors of emerging faith leaders to engage our students' questions regarding—and indictments of—our traditions' failures to engage human sexuality beyond prohibitions laced with shaming? Students bring these pressing questions into the classroom and into mentoring relationships. This student challenges us as religious leaders to pause and consider the ways that religion may be harmful:

> From an academic and practical ministerial approach and in . . . their intersections, I am most captured by the need for theologies that assist people in healing from trauma. Too often, the presence of shame within theological teaching and guidance does further harm to those who have experienced or are experiencing trauma. . . . [T]he Church has caused or been complicit in a great deal of trauma and therefore ought to be a part of the process of reconciliation and transformation.[11]

How do we assess this charge of complicity in trauma? How do we respond to this call to reconciliation and transformation?

MENTORING WITH GENDER IN MINDBODYSPIRIT

Mentoring with gender in mindbodyspirit[12] is mentoring with many questions and no easy answers; mentoring requiring us to risk moving beyond the *mind* into the fullness of, as one graduate wrote, "our, sweaty, messy beautiful bodies," and the mysteries of spirit, mentoring where we become learners as well as teachers.[13]

"Previous knowledge can be saved and used, but as physicist Thomas Kuhn points out, its domain of application becomes more restricted."[14] The question before us—one that has confronted many prior generations of religious communities—is this: how do we honor our "previous knowledge" in sacred texts and traditions while holding them in creative tension with new possibilities? Below are suggestions for mentoring with students as we faithfully hold this creative tension.

INTRAPERSONAL EXPLORATION

We begin with ourselves. Engaging questions of gender in mentoring requires time for our honest introspection. What is our relationship with our own bodies? How do issues of gender, bodies, and human sexuality impact our life and the lives of those close to us? How do we engage received religious traditions around gender, our bodies, and sexuality? What do we see and hear in current media about bodies, gender, and sexuality? What questions are we are living with?

Free writing is helpful in this process—set a time limit of 10–20 minutes daily (an alarm is helpful), and write with no concern for grammar, spelling, or punctuation and with no judgment. See what emerges. Explore who is writing/speaking about these issues from faith perspectives.

RELATIONAL ENGAGEMENT

Relationship is the foundation for cultivating trust necessary for engaging "thorny topics."

Listening

Listening to a group of young adults discuss what they see in the future, Parker Palmer remarked:

> I feel like I'm standing somewhere down the curvature of the earth, while you're close to the top of that curve looking at a horizon I can't see. But I need to know what you're seeing. Whatever's on that horizon is coming at me, as well. So please let me know what you see, and when you do, please speak loudly and clearly so I can understand what you're saying![15]

In these times of change, listening may be the wisest way of engaging gender in mentoring—listening to our students' view from closer to the horizon; listening to their experiences, their stories, their pain and joy; listening for how they envision healing; listening with humility for what we have missed along the way as well as what we have to offer.

> Listening means engaging another with embodied presence. . . . Listening is
> *sacred* in its capacity to bear witness to the life of another creature. . . .
> Listening means *hearing* another's concerns, claims, and joys so deeply that
> the conversation may be a vehicle for potential life-giving transformation.[16]

Stories

Whose stories are we in need of hearing? Whose voices are missing from our
conversations?

> [S]o much of the theology I have come to cherish is rooted in people's embod-
> ied experience—Liberation Theology, Womanist Theology, Mujerista Theolo-
> gy, etc. As a white, straight, cis-gendered, able-bodied woman, I am so com-
> pelled by these theologies as they expand my mind into a world outside of my
> own eyes, and they convict me to simply listen to those around me as stories
> and experiences are waiting to be told, and perhaps my voice isn't necessary.[17]

What are the possibilities of stories enriching our mentoring relationships?

Questions

In the Gospels, Jesus asked about 300 questions, and others asked Jesus
about 180. Guess how many questions Jesus answered—fewer than 10.[18] We
can do worse than following this example in mentoring relationships. Questions beginning with "what," "how," "when," and invitations such as "I
wonder . . ." invite exploration in ways that expository dialogue and yes or no
queries might miss. And most important of all, we need to give ourselves
permission to not know, to not have all of the answers. Maybe a true expert is
not one with all of the answers but the one with the best questions.

Engaging Imagination and Embodied Difference

Imagination and creativity potentiate renewal and transformation. Yet we
inhabit a culture driven by the engines of efficiency and production.

Recounting a particularly disturbing weekly ministry meeting prompted
this student to reflect on cultural gender biases, diversity, inherited notions of
leadership, and to *imagine* new possibilities for leading faithfully:

> This is a moment when it seems I'll never get over the white, male, heteronor-
> mative, oppressive influences that have dictated my life and contributed to my
> development as a minister and a leader.[19]
>
> *So what does it mean to imagine new possibilities for pastoral leadership*
> [italics mine] . . . that are more relational, caring, and consistent?

The best thing . . . is look to individuals who . . . lead "differently" . . . folks whose voices would not be acknowledged . . . therefore they must "lead" from a place of influence, consistency, humility, and care. It is often much more interpersonal and relational, as they usually are not . . . granted official positions of leadership.

With this in mind, maybe we *can* look to religious communities and learn about leadership . . . look at black women in the church,[20] or at LGBT folk in less-affirming spaces, or at women in evangelical churches.[21]

How might we engage our imagination? This student suggests that looking beyond the horizons of culturally constructed islands and looking toward enfleshed, divine difference may inspire us to imagine together new ways of being embodied communities of renewal and transformation.

CONCLUSION

The end returns to the beginning. I have more questions than answers, yet remain hopeful that in community, across our divinely designed diversities, we can live together into ways forward that honor our faith traditions, our human fallibility, and divine possibilities over the horizon that we cannot yet see.

QUESTIONS FOR REFLECTION

1. What assumptions about gender, sexuality, bodies, flesh informed your early faith formation, and how did these affect your embodied sense of self? How has your theology changed over time?
2. In what ways have engagement with your students informed, and possibly challenged, your theological lens on these issues?
3. What questions related to gender, faith traditions, and sacred texts are you living with?

SUGGESTED READINGS

Banaji, Mahzarin R., and A. G. Greenwald. *Blindspot: Hidden Biases of Good People*. New York: Delacorte, 2013.

Isherwood, Lisa, and David Harris. *Radical Otherness: Sociological and Theological Approaches*. New York: Routledge, 2013.

Reuther, Rosemary Radford. *Gender, Ethnicity, Religion: Views from the Other Side*. Minneapolis, MN: Augsburg Fortress, 2002.

Waddle, Ray, ed. "Sex, Gender, Power: A Reckoning [Special Issue]." *Reflections: Yale Divinity School* 105, no. 2 (Fall 2018).

West, Traci C. *Solidarity and Defiant Spirituality: Africana Lessons on Religion, Racism, and Ending Gender Violence*. New York: New York University Press, 2019.

Chapter Thirteen

Mentoring LGBTQIA Students

Cody J. Sanders

Entering into supervisory-mentoring relationships with LGBTQIA[1] theological students is a gift. The potential for rich theological reflection and cultivation of ministers in training that will gift the church with the queer ministerial presence so long denied it due to homophobic theologies and heretical worship of a hierarchical gender binary is incredible. Here, I want to help you think about ways of being a supportive presence in supervisory relationships that go beyond simply holding an affirming theological stance toward LGBTQIA people.

LEARNING TO BE A GUEST

Several weeks into my semester as a seminary student in a context of supervised ministry, my supervisor said that she had neglected to ask me about my personal life. Then she asked me if I had a girlfriend. Because I was dating another man at the time but wasn't open about this in my field placement site, my congregation, or my seminary, it was easy just to say "no" and move on.

The next week my supervisor started our session together by saying, "I realize that I made a mistake last week in our session. I asked if you had a girlfriend. I'm sorry about that. What I *should* have asked is whether you have a significant other."

I was stunned. And panicked. I really didn't know what to say. I immediately responded "no" to that question as well, and we moved on in our conversation. But twenty minutes into the supervisory session, I had the sense that this was an invitation to be known by someone that I trusted in a way that I hadn't been known before—and by a clergyperson, no less. I asked if we could return to that question. I told her that I was, in fact, in a relationship with another man.

The conversation from that point was extraordinarily supportive as my supervisor-mentor listened to my story and heard the complexities of navigating my sexual/affectional[2] identity, my relationships with family and colleagues, and the Baptist religious context into which I would soon seek ordination. My sexuality never became the *focus* of our supervisory work, but that conversation opened space for me to bring my whole self into supervision, and it felt liberating.

This vignette from my own experience as a student in a supervisory relationship is illustrative of several important factors to mentoring LGBTQIA students that may not be immediately obvious.

First, this was the first time I felt this degree of trust in a ministry supervisor whom, incidentally, I presumed to be straight. A few cues that I recall looking for as a queer ministerial student wondering how much to trust a supervisor with my personal narrative were the books my supervisors had on their shelves; the ways they spoke of sexuality and gender identity, whether in a nervous tone or in a calm matter-of-fact way; and whether their language typically *presumed* heterosexuality and cisgender[3] identities or left room for embodiments beyond these.

Second, my supervisor-mentor displayed an incredible ability and willingness to reflect upon her own mistake—in this case a heterosexist micro-aggression[4]—and to correct that unintentional slight in our following supervisory session. Her question to me in the initial session presumed heterosexuality. When she came back the next week to acknowledge this micro-invalidation, it was a signal to me that she not only knew her mistake, but she also risked being vulnerable enough with me, her student, to rectify the situation in the supervisory relationship. My trust in the relationship grew exponentially.

Third, my supervisor-mentor recognized the risk involved for *me* in answering this question. She created dialogical space for me to bring as much of my story into supervision as *I* desired, but treated me like the host of that sacred space and behaved like a guest following my lead in entering it. This is a critical skill for supervisor-mentors of LGBTQIA students.

For a long time, our usual way of naming disclosures of sexual or gender identities has been the phrase "coming out," which presumes that *secrecy* needs to be overcome and the onus of *responsibility* is on the LGBTQIA person to make an *admission of truth*. But Darnell Moore introduces the alternative metaphor of "inviting in." Moore is attentive to the lived experience of "those LGBTQIA persons whom for many reasons, such as sociocultural, neighborhood, religious, or familial contexts, may find the process of 'coming out' to be more harmful than helpful."[5] Rather, Moore says that inviting others to "come in" to our lives "functions as a means of hospitable sharing, a choice to disclose to those with whom we may feel safe disclosing to, a choice to disclose when we feel ready to do so."[6] Rather than a movement outward from the "closet," a presumed place of *secrecy*, "inviting in" offers others the opportunity to enter our "life-space" as a *sacred* place of honor for those we desire to be a part of that space.

Skillful supervisor-mentors must learn to be good guests when they have the honor of being "invited in" by an LGBTQIA student, expanding language to include diverse embodiments, recognizing mistakes and taking responsibility for them, and following the lead of the one risking the invitation into sacred life-space.

ATTENDING TO SUPERVISOR-STUDENT EMBODIMENTS

I recently taught a course on LGBTQIA pastoral care at an institution known for its stance of inclusivity toward LGBTQIA people and committed to educating clergy in competent LGBTQIA-affirming ministry. About a dozen students were in the class. In the first week, a few of the students spoke of their own LGBTQIA identities as reasons for taking the course. A week or two into the course, others had spoken and written about their LGBTQIA identities in reflective ways. It was becoming clearer to me that the majority of the students in the class identified as LGBTQIA. Finally, several weeks into the course, the *one* straight cisgender student in the class outed herself.

This student was the *only* person in the class who identified as both straight and cisgender. We laughed together at the recognition that it was the straight cisgender person who finally had to out herself, turning the tables on her typical experience reflecting the dominant norm. We reflected together on her experience as the minority sexual and gender embodiment in the class. And we talked about what it was like for the LGBTQIA students to discover that they were in the *majority* in this learning space.

Joretta Marshall asks "what it means for students and their learning to have someone—or no one—who looks more like them or who represents something about their particularity of difference."[7] For many of the LGBTQIA students in class, the experience was liberative. It was the first time they had been in a majority inside any classroom. For some, it was the first time they had taken a course from a queer-identified professor. And for most, it was the first time they had taken a course focused on aspects of *their* embodied experience as LGBTQIA people.

When embodiments of difference pertaining to affectional orientation or gender identity differ between supervisors and students, an opportunity emerges for critical reflection on the power differentials that exist in the learning environment, how these differences exist also in the ministry context, and how students can reflect upon embodiment as an important site of theological inquiry.

NAVIGATING PAIN AND CONFLICT IN MINISTRY SETTINGS

No matter how affirming and supportive your supervision, do not take for granted that the LGBTQIA student you are mentoring is free of conflict and pain around the student's affectional orientation or gender identity in the ministry setting. Even affirming settings can be fraught with painful encounters.

For example, a congregant in a newly affirming congregation says to a gay ministerial student, "I'm just so glad this church has *you* as our example of a gay minister. You're just so *normal*, and it's easier for us to accept you." Or a straight parishioner to a lesbian intern says, "I don't really see you as lesbian. I just see you as a person, and I don't really care what you do in bed." Or a trans student becomes the go-to person that congregants approach to ask questions about trans experience, all asked from an affirming perspective, but inappropriate to the student's role in the congregation.

LGBTQIA-competent supervision should allow space for students to process painful experiences that may not rise to the level of outright insult or degradation but bespeak the latent heterosexism and genderism that emerge even in overtly affirming contexts. These micro-aggressive communications may not seem like a very big deal in an isolated sense, but they can touch tender places in students' theological world. Theological discourse has the potential to strengthen aggressive and micro-aggressive communications toward LGBTQIA people by setting these heterosexist and transphobic communications within an ultimate context, lending them spiritual weight to wound differently than in nontheological contexts. This requires space to risk processing these wounds carefully in dialogue with a supportive mentor that the student invites in to this sacred life-space.

LEARNING TO LEARN FROM LGBTQIA LIVES

As in many of our ecclesial contexts, so, too, with our mentoring relationships, we often stop with an affirming stance toward LGBTQIA people. When we've had the critical conversations and discerned our way through prayerful dialogue and arrived at a place of greater inclusion of LGBTQIA people into the structures of community and belonging—baptism, marriage, ordination, and so forth—we feel a (false) sense of completion.

Joretta Marshall argues, "Eager allies sometimes have difficulty listening deeply to the knowledge of 'others' in ways that fully engage both their existential experiences and encourage disciplined thinking and reflection on that experience."[8] Beyond affirming the affectional and gender identities of the students you supervise in ministry, important work is yet to be done toward developing "compassionate curiosity" into the experience of LGBTQIA students.[9] This isn't a curiosity for curiosity's sake. It is a curiosity that seeks to engage existential experiences of LGBTQIA people fully; curiosity that emerges from an epistemological stance that holds that LGBTQIA lives are sites of *theological wisdom.*

One of the most powerful acts of affirmation for my humanity as a gay person in a supervisory setting occurred in a clinical supervision group in which I was a student not open about my sexuality. The other students in the class were debating some aspect of sexuality in a very overtly non-LGBTQIA-affirming manner when our straight cisgender supervisor-mentor stopped the conversation and told the entirety of the group of students that she believed any professional stance that did not support and affirm LGBTQIA people would be a detriment to our vocations in caregiving careers. If we couldn't address this limitation, she said, then we should seriously consider other career possibilities. I had never heard anyone in a supervisory or professorial role express such strong insistence on the dignity and worth of LGBTQIA lives. I was heartened beyond belief.

I wonder what would happen if we developed such strong stances beyond simple inclusion—as important as that is—to suggest with similar authority that if any of us is not compassionately curious about what we can learn *theologically* from the lives of LGBTQIA people, then perhaps theological education and ministerial supervision may be the wrong vocational path for us. We certainly would be moving well on our way beyond the homophobic theologies and heretical worship of a hierarchical gender binary that have so long denied our churches the gifts of LGBTQIA ministers.

QUESTIONS FOR REFLECTION

1. Questions on inviting in: How does your supervisory style or typical educational process either presume heterosexuality and cisgender identity, or make room for the possibility of students inviting you in to their diversity of affectional orientations and gender identities? How does this come through in your language? In your educational resources?

2. Questions on supervisor-student embodiment: Have your students ever had LGBTQIA supervisor-mentors or teachers? Have they had supervisor-mentors and teachers who recognized LGBTQIA people as sites of significant wisdom and generative theological imagination? What differences do you imagine these experiences making for your students' learning?

3. Questions on learning from LGBTQIA lives: What have you learned as a practitioner of ministry from the lives and experiences of LGBTQIA people? How can you imagine helping your LGBTQIA students see their own lives as valuable sources of theological wisdom? How can you similarly help straight and cisgender students develop such compassionate curiosity?

SUGGESTED READINGS AND RESOURCES

Cheng, Patrick S. *Rainbow Theology: Bridging Race, Sexuality, and Spirit*. New York: Seabury, 2013.

Marshall, Joretta L. "Differences, Dialogues, and Discourses: From Sexuality to Queer Theory in Learning and Teaching." *Journal of Pastoral Theology* 19, no. 2 (2009): 29–47.

Sanders, Cody J. *Queer Lessons for Churches on the Straight and Narrow: What All Christians Can Learn from LGBTQ Lives*. Macon, GA: Faithlab, 2013.

Tanis, Justin. *Trans-Gender: Theology, Ministry and Communities of Faith*, 2nd ed. Eugene, OR: Wipf and Stock, 2018.

Tilsen, Julie. *Therapeutic Conversations with Queer Youth: Transcending Homonormativity and Constructing Preferred Identities*. New York: Jason Aronson, 2013.

Chapter Fourteen

Trauma-Informed Mentoring

Lia Scholl

Trauma-informed mentoring assumes that your intern has trauma—and plans accordingly.

Experts say that as many as 70 percent of people experience some type of traumatic event at least once in their lives.[1] Not all of those people develop trauma, but many of them do.

There are no rules about what causes trauma. And no definition of trauma explains why some react to underlying causes with trauma and others escape unscathed. Peter Levine in *Waking the Tiger: Healing Trauma* writes, "No matter how frightening an event may seem, not everyone who experiences it will be traumatized."[2] Trauma is highly individualized.

Trauma is how our body, mind, and spirit respond to violence, illness, or loss, either in a single event or series of events, that has happened to us or loved ones. Recent studies have shown that we may carry generational trauma, too. We may or may not remember the underlying causes. According to Bessel Van Der Kolk, MD, "Trauma, by definition, is unbearable. . . . It takes tremendous energy to keep functioning while carrying the memory of terror, and the shame of utter weakness and vulnerability."[3]

All trauma survivors move through pain, some with "dirty pain" as Resmaa Menakem calls it, exposing others to their pain through denial, avoidance, and blame. "Dirty pain" creates more pain and trauma. But "healing trauma involves recognizing, accepting, and moving through pain—clean pain." Menakem says, "Clean pain is about choosing integrity over fear. It is about letting go of what is familiar but harmful, finding the best parts of yourself and making a leap—with no guarantee of safety or praise."[4]

What does trauma look like in your intern? The amygdala controls trauma responses, which can be more nuanced than just fight, flight, and freeze—but that's a great place to start. Flight may look like an unexpected retreat, or an untimely escape. One intern I worked with just disappeared when trig-gered—she dashed toward the restroom and didn't come out for a long time.

Trauma also might look like a freeze response. One intern would "blank out" when we were talking, sometimes for as long as two or three minutes. Freeze responses often require that you repeat your question. They even may require that you give your intern more time to respond to questions.

Trauma can also look like "fight." In my experience, fight looks more like overreaction than an actual fight. One intern, in a conversation that had nothing to do with her work or accusing her of anything, yelled out "I feel attacked" in the middle of a staff meeting.

Whatever you do, don't ask your intern to "tell her story." A myth used to be that telling the story over and over would take the sting out of the story, and therefore, heal the trauma. It's not true. Telling the story activates the amygdala and has the effect of reliving the traumatic event, over and over again. If you find that your mentee is telling you the story, nicely remind her that she doesn't have to repeat it, that you know bad stuff happened, and you trust her story.

Ten principles of trauma-informed services guide my thinking with men-toring relationships, adapted from the work of Denise E. Elliott, Paula Bjela-jac, Roger D. Fallot, Laurie S. Markoff, and Beth Lover Reed.[5]

1. Trauma-informed mentoring recognizes the impact of violence and victimization on development and coping strategies.

Survivors with trauma often develop coping strategies that include pro-crastination on uncomfortable projects, covering up imagined failures and difficulties, or exhibiting overly solicitous, even sycophantic behavior. These are learned, adaptive behaviors that increase the trauma survivor's feeling of safety.

However, these same behaviors can interfere with the mentoring relation-ship. Instead of focusing on these behaviors as *wrong*, the mentor can focus on them as *adaptive*, or even maladaptive, and with gentle honesty point out that the behaviors are not necessary.

2. Trauma-informed mentoring identifies recovery from trauma as an ongoing goal for a minister.

The goal of mentoring ministers is not to "fix" them, but to help them be better ministers, even if only incrementally. The way that traumatized minis-ters become better ministers is to work to heal their own trauma.

Even though mentoring is not a therapeutic model, mentors have the opportunity to employ some of those therapeutic models as part of their approach. If possible, give your intern access to a helper and listener—whether it be traditional therapy, spiritual direction, or some sort of therapeu-tic body work.

Creating new relationships and learning new skills will surface issues, and providing a safer space will give your intern a place to talk about where her own trauma is triggered in the work—even with her mentor. That "safer space" should be outside of your mentoring relationship. You're the supervisor, not the therapist.

3. Trauma-informed mentoring employs an empowerment model.

The foundations of an empowerment model rely on buy-in from the mentee, mutually agreed-upon goals, and supportive resources to help the mentee reach his goals.

In each of my mentoring meetings, the intern always answers these questions:

• What are your successes in this week's work?
• What are your challenges coming up in the next week?
• How can I support you in meeting those challenges?

In these three questions, we affirm the intern meeting his own goals, and celebrate with him, we see his goals for the next week, and we can find appropriate resources to help him meet those goals.

4. Trauma-informed mentoring strives to maximize the mentee's choices and control over her work.

I once had a student intern who was preaching for the first time and brought in her sermon to discuss it. It was a very angry sermon. Preaching it was ill advised, and could have broken some relationships.

With a very short time line, I stepped in to help with a rewrite of the sermon. In hindsight, I realize that I overstepped both my authority and the intern's right to control her own work.

In the church, sometimes it's difficult to maximize a mentee's choices and control over her work, but it should be a goal. If I were to face this situation again, I would have removed the time limitations by pushing the mentee's sermon off a few weeks and had her rewrite it.

5. Trauma-informed mentoring is based on a relational collaboration.

At best, the work we do as mentor is a relational collaboration—and that relationship building can help heal the trauma that the intern has experienced. This is especially true of those who have experienced harm by the church. By honoring our mentees, by being trustworthy relational partners, healing can happen.

6. Trauma-informed mentoring creates an atmosphere that is respectful of survivors' need for safety, respect, and acceptance.

Let's face it. The church is not always a safe place filled with respect and acceptance. My interns have attended meetings where church members have high levels of anxiety and have scapegoated a minister or criticized one another. We can't always manufacture that type of space.

However, we can excuse our interns from those types of meetings. We can give and receive feedback about the meetings in a way that is safe. We can speak up for our interns in the case of unsafe interactions.

I have had a couple of interns who have faced micro-aggressions in my church. In those situations, addressing the safety and respect of my interns with the one who created harm has been very important, even though it risks the alienation of the offender.

We cannot make a perfect place for our students to learn, but we should try.

7. Trauma-informed mentoring emphasizes the strengths of our mentees, highlighting adaptations over symptoms and resilience over pathology.

Remember that trauma is, by nature, unbearable. And yet, your intern has survived it. He may have created some maladaptive behaviors in order to survive. As noted above, they can be avoidant techniques, such as denial, delay, or withdrawal.

Make it a fundamental practice to highlight those behaviors as "survival tools," and remind your mentee that those very tools helped him survive. But as good as they have worked in the past, they are not good survival tools for this time.

The best thing I know to help a trauma survivor who is stuck in old behaviors is to brainstorm new ones. You can say, "I noticed that you use denial as a defense when you were late on Sunday. That may have worked well to keep you out of trouble in the past. Using denial has probably been a good tactic. However, it's not working in this particular setting. Is there a way we can work on another behavior?"

Then lead your intern into a discussion of "could have's." You could have said, "Yes. I am late. I am sorry." Or you could have texted when you realized you were running late. What else could you have done?

8. The goal of trauma-informed mentoring is to minimize the possibilities of r-traumatization.

In my experience, some people in our churches are abusive. Most ministers can point out the abusers in their congregation. It also has been my experience that abusers often build relationships with people who have been abused in the past. I don't know why this happens, but I've seen it in congregations where I've served.

I believe, fundamentally, that interns should be protected from those individuals in our congregations. This may mean coaching your intern to avoid those folks. It may mean tagging along when they're interacting together. Some trauma survivors can be vulnerable to attack, and staying aware and tuned in is important.

9. Trauma-informed mentoring strives to be culturally competent and to understand all mentees in the context of their lived experiences.

I've found that one of the most profound discussions to have with mentees is a discussion about the family system in their family of origin. Connecting those dots to their current situation and their experience of the church is very important and will serve them in ministry for years to come.

Cultural and religious understanding of their lived experience is important, too. Many of the young ministers I know have left evangelicalism that was intolerant of their sexuality or gender expression. Some young ministers come from systems that are replete with abuse. These are important understandings for interns finding their way in a new system, and helpful as we guide them through them.

10. Trauma-informed mentoring solicits input from mentees and involves them in designing and evaluating their work.

Every step of the way in trauma-informed mentoring means stepping lightly and asking for permission, feedback, and ways to improve. And although it may feel like mentoring with kid gloves, in reality, your interns already have shown such resiliency, they likely will survive you, too.

Here are some ways you can create a safer space where your interns can thrive:

- Institute a consent policy for all touching in your office and church. Trauma survivors (and people without trauma, too) should not have to endure physical touch that they do not want.
- Create a trauma-informed toolbox in your office. My toolbox has squeeze toys galore, from squeezable jiggly dinosaur toys and stretchable wiggle worms, to soft bouncy balls with lights. These toys help my interns stay present in hard conversations.
- A white noise machine in your office is a great tool for confidentiality and privacy in conversation. It also mutes the unexpected noises outside your office.
- Always have water on hand, primarily because taking a sip of water can give a person experiencing trauma a moment to relax.
- Use low lighting and low voices in your one-on-one time with your mentor. Many trauma survivors are triggered by loud noises and voices.
- Don't put a desk between you and your mentee, but instead work at a table, emphasizing the relational nature of the mentoring relationship.
- Talking about serious subjects is difficult when you sit across from one another. Try walking or driving at the time that you talk about difficult topics.
- Get comfortable with long silences. Sometimes people need a minute to gather their thoughts or their scattered mind. I often find an excuse to step out of the room—a bathroom break or grabbing a water.
- Breathe. When the amygdala is in panic mode, the off switch is the breath. If you take a deep breath, anyone sitting with you likely will take one, too.

It's just like yawning: it's infectious. Sometimes, though, it takes a direct "Take a deep breath with me" statement. That's OK, too.

Help your interns understand how trauma affects all of us, even if they are not trauma survivors.

QUESTIONS FOR REFLECTION

1. Have you yourself experienced trauma? What were the strategies (maladaptive or adaptive) that helped you survive?
2. Has there been a time in your own ministry where you have seen a congregant in deep trauma? What were the things that helped you navigate through it?
3. Vicarious trauma, which is the emotional weight of bearing others' trauma, can be a problem in ministry. Have you found ways to release others' pain?

SUGGESTED READINGS

Elliott, Denise E., Paula Bjelajac, Roger D. Fallot, Laurie S. Markoff, and Beth Lover Reed. "Trauma-Informed or Trauma-Denied: Principles and Implementation of Trauma-Informed Services for Women." *Journal of Community Psychology* 33, no. 4 (2005): 461–77.
Levine, Peter A. *Waking the Tiger: Healing Trauma.* Berkeley, CA: North Atlantic Books, 1997.
Menakem, Resmaa. *My Grandmother's Hands: Racialized Trauma and the Pathway to Mending Our Hearts and Bodies.* Las Vegas, NV: Central Recovery Press, 2017.
Van Der Kolk, Bessel. *The Body Keeps the Score: Brain, Mind, and the Body in the Healing of Trauma.* New York: Penguin, 2014.

Chapter Fifteen

Mentoring for Leadership in Nonprofit Settings

John Senior and Margaret Elliott

Your work as a supervisor-mentor to ministry interns who want to learn the skills and practices of nonprofit leadership is critical. Traditional seminary and divinity school curricula do not always include many resources for preparing religious leadership in faith-based or secular nonprofit organizations. But there is no doubt that the resources of theological education offer much to position excellent leaders in nonprofit spaces. For example, theological traditions contain the moral resources that help leaders better articulate the mission and vision of nonprofit organizations to various stakeholders. In another example, training in pastoral care prepares leaders who engage clients and guests of nonprofit organizations with creativity and empathy. Your role as supervisor-mentor is critical in helping ministry interns to operationalize their theological education to prepare them for leadership in nonprofit organizations. We have identified four themes to help you guide your mentoring of ministry interns: walking the landscapes, staying connected to your organization's mission and vision, leading from abundance, and responding to structural injustice.

WALKING THE LANDSCAPES

Margaret shares a story of her first experience working professionally in a nonprofit organization in southwest Virginia that provided a range of caring services to older adults. Margaret investigated complaints of residents in long-term care facilities. She offered in-service training opportunities for the facility staff members. The training showed staff members that Margaret understood the difficulty of their positions. It also helped to build trust so that future complaints were handled with genuine cooperation and collaboration.

Margaret describes the executive director for whom she worked as excellent, one who had a lot of experience and was well-known in the community, and who had a gift for collaborating with other local organizations. Margaret made it a point to ask lots of questions, and her ED was happy to answer them. Margaret says: "We used to take walks together at lunchtime, and she told me about the organization. I knew more about the organization than anybody did because we walked at lunchtime, and I asked questions about how one does the work. So I was learning as I went along." The ED's main gift as a supervisor-mentor, Margaret said, was that she was willing to share information, all the time, about the organization.

Like all interns, students who are serving in nonprofit organizations for the first time will, of course, need to learn the ropes: learn how to navigate their daily work and tasks with proficiency. Often, student interns enter a nonprofit setting without any prior coursework to prepare them for nonprofit leadership. So, they will need to ask a lot of questions about how things work, and you will need to be prepared to answer them. Like Margaret's first ED, it will be important to find ways of inviting students to ask questions, to meet them in their curiosity about your work, your organization, and the kinds of know-how required to lead it.

By taking lunchtime walks with her ED, Margaret also was learning various landscapes of the organization she served. She learned the literal geographical landscape, situating this organization's services in relationship to the persons and communities who needed them, and how spatial relationships conditioned the ways in which services were delivered. She also learned from her mentor about the landscape of structural injustice in southwest Virginia—that is, the conditions that create obstacles to the proper care of older adults in that particular region. Finally, Margaret learned about the landscape of nonprofit work—and in particular, about the many creative ways that nonprofit organizations in her region partnered and cooperated on projects and programs to better respond to the challenges present in that space.

Key questions: What are the opportunities for you to introduce your intern to the various "landscapes" in which your organization and its work are situated? How might you help your intern to reflect on the contexts of your organization's work?

STAYING CONNECTED TO YOUR ORGANIZATION'S
MISSION AND VISION

Several years ago, one of John's students served as an intern in a nonprofit organization whose mission is to provide quality clothing to women without access to professional attire required for a successful job search. This student initially was overwhelmed by what she described as a "chaotic environment" in the workplace. The workspace seemed disorganized. The communication between staff and clients was at various times and in various ways confusing. It wasn't always clear to the student what her day-to-day roles and responsibilities were. Like many small nonprofits, this organization made do on a shoestring: personnel, funding, time, and energy always are limited, and the need is always great. This student learned to lean into the "chaos" of this particular organization. As a result, she learned much that summer about finding the rhythm of nonprofit work under challenging conditions.

One of the most relentlessly pressing conditions of nonprofit leadership is the challenge of navigating a world of endless need in an environment of limited resources, competing responses to needs, and variously interested stakeholders. And let's not forget the challenges of day-to-day bureaucratic and administrative work that keep a nonprofit organization going. This work of navigation can be exhausting, in part because you as a nonprofit leader may feel on some days that you are doing everything in your organization BUT the work you feel really called and energized to do. Such an environment can make it difficult for any nonprofit leader to be motivated to roll out of bed every morning and show up for work—whatever that looks like on any particular day.

Perhaps this question, then, is a helpful way to identify a key challenge of mentoring ministry leaders learning to serve in nonprofit settings: how do you help emerging nonprofit leaders stay connected to the energy and passion that drive your vocation as well as your organization's mission and vision? "Vision" here means a picture of the world when the nonprofit organization's key concerns have been addressed successfully. How would the world look if your organization's work were brought to completion? Or put differently: what would the world look like if the day came when your organization could close because its work no longer was necessary? "Mission" means the primary activities (programs, services, etc.) in which your organization engages in order to fulfill its vision. What is your organization doing in order to bring about its vision? Mission and vision often are articulated in succinct statements (or one statement) that nonprofit organizations use to frame their work and make decisions about the kinds of programming they will offer, funding they will pursue, internal organizational practices, and so forth.

As our student's experience illustrates, it is not always easy to stay connected to and energized by your organization's mission and vision amid the day-to-day challenges of leading a nonprofit organization. As a nonprofit leader, how do you nurture this connection? Of course, this question is deeply related to your own gifts, talents, and opportunities for continued growth as a leader. Some everyday tasks and projects align well with your gifts and energies, and you may find it easier to connect these with your commitment to the bigger vision of your organization. Others may be more challenging. Perhaps some seasons of your work wear you down, and you have to be intentional about finding ways to reconnect yourself both to your own energies and passions as well as those that drive your organization's vision and mission. Maybe you find time to learn the stories of persons that your organization serves. Or maybe in challenging seasons you find ways to change up your work so that you see different sides of your organization's impact. How do you stay connected in these ways? And what guidance would you offer your interns about aligning their own gifts and talents for nonprofit leadership with the organization's mission and vision, as well as being open to continued growth as a leader?

Key questions: How do you stay connected to your organization's mission and vision amid the many demands of everyday nonprofit work? And how can you help your interns to do the same?

LEADING FROM ABUNDANCE

One of the main lessons that Margaret learned in that same nonprofit in southwest Virginia was that, as she puts it, communities "that did not have many resources work so much better together, because they had to." She often thinks about this lesson in her current position as the executive director of a major nonprofit in Winston-Salem, North Carolina. Her current organization certainly values collaboration, but because it is better resourced, collaboration is not as pressing a need as it was in southwest Virginia. Margaret also learned in this early experience to address problems in ways that would provide clear benefits to all parties involved and regularly draws on these lessons to promote collaboration in her current leadership position.

Another way to think about these questions is to understand your organization's vision and mission as its commitment to a world defined by abundance rather than scarcity. Asset-based community development models begin with the assumption that local communities have valuable resources that citizens can mobilize to address issues of shared concern. That is, they begin with the assumption of abundance that empowers local agency rather than lack that requires external response. Similarly, broad-based community organizing traditions often draw a distinction between an understanding of the "world as it is" and the "world as it should be." These traditions remind us that it is all too easy to allow the world as it is to define our expectations and aspirations for our lives.

The "world as it is" is defined by particular configurations of power that work to maintain these configurations as they are. The configurations of power that make "the world as it is" work hard to promote the idea that resources are scarce, and "the world as it is" has already arranged those resources in the best way possible. But nothing is inevitable about "the world as it is," and we have no reason to think that resources are so scarce that injustice has to be a norm. Community organizing models assume a world of abundance and attempt to carefully draw an incremental, strategically nuanced roadmap from the "world as it is" to the "world as it should be," from scarcity to abundance. Similarly, a nonprofit organization's mission and vision statement(s) identifies a picture of the world as it should be.

Key questions: How do you navigate a world often defined by scarcity from the perspective of a vision of the world defined by abundance? How do you bring a vision of the "world as it should be" alive in your day-to-day work in nonprofit leadership? Which habits and practices can you introduce to your intern that promote leadership from a place of abundance rather than scarcity?

RESPONDING TO STRUCTURAL INJUSTICE

A third-year master of divinity student who served as an intern at a local poverty services nonprofit spent a portion of her time working in the new client intake process. From the beginning of her experience, the student noticed important differences between the clients whom the organization served and the staff and volunteers who managed the intake process. She wrote: "After working at [this organization] for several months, I noticed that more often than not, the client and the volunteer lived in completely different worlds. They had totally different life experiences, present realities, trials, etc." Most of this organization's clients live in poverty, while the vast majority of staff and volunteers do not, our student noted. Indeed, most volunteers are retirees who have the time, resources, and leisure to serve the organization.

The student noticed parallel disparities in the racial identities of clients and volunteers: "While the majority of the people that we serve are people of color, the majority of our volunteers (especially the interviewers) are white. So more often than not, when a client comes in and is explaining their crisis, they are talking to someone who not only looks different than them, but also lives in a completely different reality than they do."

These observations became fodder for a project that the student completed around her internship work. Her framing question for the project was "How can nonprofit leaders build meaningful relationships with people living in poverty, while also acknowledging the different levels of power and privilege?" This student's presentation explored gender, racial, and socioeconomic disparities not only between clients and nonprofit service providers but also within nonprofit organizations, between organizational leaders, staff, and volunteers. All of these dynamics are, of course, not simply a question of diversity and representation; they are at bottom an issue of power and privilege, dynamics that are created and maintained through complex and interwoven social, cultural, political, and historical realities.

This student's experience reflects a deep tension in nonprofit space, and thus an important condition of mentoring emerging nonprofit leaders. The nonprofit sector reflects all of the complex dynamics of structural injustice that condition experiences of race, gender, and class in the United States. When I refer to "structure," I follow theologian Cynthia Moe-Lobeda, who identifies structure with social arrangements, "be they political, economic, cultural, military, or other," that are ordered in ways that "enable some people to have vastly more access than other people to material goods and other resources, tools for acquiring them, and power for determining the terms of life in common."[1] "Structural injustice" refers to the ways in which these complex, impersonal, and interlocking structures deny the conditions of flourishing to, or even actively enact violence upon, human beings and the natural order.

How, then, does the nonprofit sector reflect the structural conditions of injustice in the U.S. context? Nonprofit organizations are often understood to attend to "gaps" in the provision of basic goods and services left by market and government systems. This logic suggests an obvious tension between charity and justice: gaps in provision do exist, of course, and they must be filled. But assigning to the nonprofit sector the work of filling them threatens to reinforce a paradigm of provision that perpetuates the very structural problems that create "gaps" in the first place.

Similarly, some have critiqued the "nonprofit industrial complex," a shorthand for describing the co-optation of the nonprofit sector, especially through its funding structures, by those who control forms of economic, political, and cultural power.[2] Moreover, as governments have gotten "smaller" in the past half century, the nonprofit sector in the U.S. context has taken increasing responsibility for the provision of basic goods and services. Accelerating especially with the Nixon and Reagan administrations, federal, state, and local governments have ceded to the nonprofit sector the responsibility for provision, leading to "the nonprofitization of the welfare state."[3] Increasingly, then, the nonprofit sector is doing more than simply filling gaps; it has become a primary institutional arrangement through which basic goods and services are provided.

This student's experiences of navigating diversity of identities and disparities in power can be seen against the backdrop of these structural conditions. That is, the phenomenon of relatively wealthy, privileged, empowered, and leisured white staff and volunteers serving clients who inhabit marginalized and vulnerable identities reflects the many ways that political, economic, cultural and other realities, outside of the control and agency of any one person or group, work to create the conditions of these encounters. The work of any nonprofit organization in complex ways participates in, in some ways reinforces, and also critiques and even works to dismantle structural conditions of injustice. Good mentors, then, will invite emerging nonprofit leaders to think through what it means for your organization to be situated within these structural realities and how your interns think about these issues, both with respect to their work in your internship setting and in relationship to their own unfolding sense of vocation.

QUESTIONS FOR REFLECTION

1. How does our organization both participate in and also critically respond to structural conditions of injustice? What are ways that you can invite your intern to process this complexity?
2. Where might there be opportunities for our organization to respond in creative ways to structural injustice, and how do your interns think about those opportunities?
3. How are the interns interpreting their experiences doing the work of justice in your organization with their sense of purpose and vocation?

SUGGESTED READINGS

Garry, Joan. *Joan Garry's Guide to Nonprofit Leadership: Because Nonprofits Are Messy.* Hoboken, NJ: John Wiley & Sons, 2017.

INCITE! *The Revolution Will Not Be Funded: Beyond the Nonprofit Industrial Complex.* Durham, NC: Duke University Press, 2017.

Reich, Rob. *Just Giving: Why Philanthropy Is Failing and How It Can Do Better.* Princeton, NJ: Princeton University Press, 2018.

Chapter Sixteen

Mentoring for Ministry in Chaplaincy Settings

Amy Canosa

"How am I supposed to offer care to this dying Jewish woman I've never even met? I'm a twenty-three-year-old Baptist woman! I'm not prepared for this!" This is what my exasperated student, Cara,[1] exclaimed as she came barreling into my office on her second full day at the hospital. "This is all new territory for me, and I don't know what I'm doing!"

Unique opportunities for learning and education come through chaplaincy experiences that are quite different from traditional ministry settings. To be a religious person in a secular or multi-faith space invites you to reflect more deeply upon your faith and develop curiosity and awareness of how others experience and live their faith.

If this is your students' first chaplaincy context, they likely will need to process several questions with you:

- how to live into their religious role while in a secular or multi-faith setting
- what the difference is between "visitation" and a "pastoral care/chaplain visit"
- how to offer care to someone who is culturally very different than they are
- how to speak to pastoral needs that may or may not line up with their own theological beliefs or values
- how to respect and maintain boundaries and confidentiality

Several of these questions played a role in the great angst of my student, Cara. As her supervisor-mentor it was important for me to remember and be attentive to my initial fears and insecurities as I began this work. I have found it helpful to normalize students' anxiety and acknowledge to them my own bumps along the way. Sharing how your learning has been ongoing can help lower some of the initial anxiety your students may experience.

RELIGIOUS ROLE

How long did it take you to really understand the role of the chaplain? Oftentimes it can take some time before students really "get" what we do. Added to that difficulty is the challenge that even in our ministry settings the patients/clients/individuals also may be unclear. In the hospital setting, students have shared that they've been asked on numerous occasions if they are a local minister trying to win "new converts." Your students likely will struggle with knowing how to understand themselves and how to express what they can offer to individuals. I have found it important to give students space to reflect on how they plan to "show up" in a space, even down to what clothes they will wear.

Paul, a second-year Episcopalian student, struggled over whether to wear his cleric collar while in the hospital setting. As his supervisor-mentor, I invited him to reflect on what the potential pros and cons of wearing it might be. He recognized that when he wore the collar he felt more secure in his role, and it helped him feel more confident in his pastoral identity.

However, he also was worried that some people might see his collar, assume things about his beliefs or practices, and be "turned off" by it. He also wondered about carrying his Book of Common Prayer around, as again it brought him comfort. As his supervisor-mentor, I felt it important to allow Paul to wrestle with these questions, rather than giving him a quick and easy response. Model for students the same kind of curiosity you hope they engage with patients. I wondered with Paul what it might be like to try different approaches over his internship and see what happened. Over the next couple of weeks, Paul opted to wear his collar some days and leave it home on others. He also alternated between his Bible and the Book of Common Prayer. Ultimately his anxiety and focus on himself lessened, and his energy began to focus more on the patients and their needs. You may feel anxious giving your student space to try on different personas and styles. In Paul's case, the freedom to try on different ways of being helped him to find more comfort in his skin and to reflect more on his developing pastoral identity.

DIFFERENCE IN VISITATION AND PASTORAL VISIT

One of the first things I hear from students who either have served as pastor or have participated in a parish-based field education experience is that the kind of visits they do as a chaplain are different than church visitation. They will come to you needing help discerning the difference. My sense is that sometimes what they are experiencing early on is the difference in offering sympathy versus empathy. Brené Brown, in a very helpful video,[2] highlights four attributes of empathy used by a nursing scholar, Theresa Wiseman.

1. to be able to see the world as others see it (perspective taking)
2. to be nonjudgmental
3. to understand another person's feelings
4. to communicate the understanding of that person's feelings

You can view this video clip with your students to help them begin to imagine how to come alongside another person. For me, at its core, chaplaincy is all about journeying alongside individuals during some of their most difficult and challenging days. Your students likely will struggle with coming alongside others. Our tendency is to lead or carry or even pull people to places of hope. We also then tend to avoid engaging sad or angry feelings or the more negative aspects of a person's life. I hear students say often, "I just want to *give them* some hope." We tend to want to be "fixers" and to find some way to alleviate pain. The reality is that often we can't do much to "fix" a situation.

We often talk about "ministry of presence" in the context of chaplaincy ministry. Monica Coleman offers, "The ministry of presence asserts that there is power—divine power—in just showing up and sticking around. It suggests that the incarnation is more important than the Word."[3] Often students struggle to understand how "showing up" can be comforting, and filled with hope. Below are two quotes I invite students to consider.

> When we honestly ask ourselves which person in our lives means the most to us, we often find that it is those who, instead of giving advice, solutions, or cures, have chosen rather to share our pain and touch our wounds with a warm and tender hand. The friend who can be silent with us in a moment of despair or confusion, who can stay with us in an hour of grief and bereavement, who can tolerate not knowing, not curing, not healing and face with us the reality of our powerlessness, that is a friend who cares.[4]

> Don't say it's not really so bad. Because it is. Death is awful, demonic. If you think your task as comforter is to tell me that really, all things considered, it's not too bad, you do not sit with me in my grief but place yourself off in the distance away from me. Over there, you are of no help.[5]

After viewing the Brené Brown video, invite your student to think about the persons who have journeyed alongside them. Ask:

- Who has been most helpful to you? What did they do that was helpful?

• Have you ever felt someone was trying to be helpful, but it didn't help? What were they doing? What can you learn about that in this context?

As a caregiver, I continually ask myself why I am offering this or that pastoral intervention. Is it my need to offer hope or comfort, because I am uncomfortable, or has the individual before me expressed a need that I can meet? Chaplains always must be assessing how our social location, beliefs, and feelings are informing the care we are offering.

CULTURE

If this is their first chaplaincy setting, your students likely will encounter people from varying religious traditions and spiritual and cultural practices. Understanding one's social and cultural location is essential because our culture has helped to create and define our meaning-making framework and has shaped how we see the world. Culture is the shared patterns of behavior and interactions, cognitive constructs, and understandings that are learned through socialization.

Individuals learn and engage differently because of their cultural location. It is important for you to recognize and help your students understand how their social location, judgments, and implicit bias impact how they experience those for whom they are seeking to provide care. Be mindful of how your social location impacts how you see and experience your students. Several resources that have been helpful and challenging to me are listed below.

PASTORAL VERSUS TRADITIONAL RESPONSE

Have you been asked to provide a ritual or sacrament that was outside your religious tradition? Or were you asked to perform a ritual before you reached clerical status that would authorize you to administer the sacraments? How did this make you feel? What caused these feelings? What helped you determine what to do?

Your students likely will wrestle with similar questions when someone makes a pastoral request that is outside their own beliefs or practices. This was definitely true for Mark, a mid-twenties male Orthodox student who was asked by an Episcopalian patient to offer Communion. Mark's tradition limits who is able to receive the sacrament only to those who also are Orthodox. Mark's initial instinct was to come to me and say, "I can't do this." As a supervisor-mentor, you will want to listen for where your students are feeling challenge or resistance and work to support them in their discomfort.

I invited Mark to reflect on why he couldn't offer Communion. It was important to clarify with him that I was not asking him to perform the ritual/ sacrament, but to reflect on his tradition and culture, and his discomfort. This invitation to Mark, to slow down, sit, and reflect, led to his growing aware-ness about tensions he felt between the historic traditions and values of his church and the unique pastoral needs of an individual. Mark reflected on his role as an Orthodox deacon and his role as a chaplain in a hospital context. Ultimately, Mark decided that he could and should offer Communion to this woman because he felt his holy calling was to connect people to God. Though his views on Communion were different than hers, he saw and could appreciate Communion as a ritual that would offer her peace and connection to her faith in the midst of her suffering. He recognized that though he likely would not offer her Communion in his congregation, his role in the hospital created space for more flexibility in his response.

It was important for me not to rush Mark's process and reflection. Had I just told Mark to offer Communion or given him a pass not to, he would have missed out on some fruitful theological work that enabled him to continue to grow in his pastoral identity and authority. As a supervisor-mentor, you will want to continue to be attentive to your own feelings and beliefs around which rituals and sacraments you offer and how to help your students come to their own feelings and beliefs.

GROWTH AND BOUNDARIES

At the conclusion of Cara's internship, she acknowledged how rich the expe-rience had been and marveled how much she had learned while working in the hospital context. As someone planning to serve as a parish minister after graduation, she acknowledged how her experience in the hospital prepared her well for her church. As a young person, she felt like she had added five years' experience. We laughed about her initial burst into my office and celebrated the hard work she had engaged in in this setting.

Cara acknowledged that one of the most difficult—and yet most help-ful—aspects of the internship was maintaining confidentiality and boundaries. After hard days, she found herself wanting to tell her roommates all of the gory details of the hospital. When one of her fellow church mem-bers asked her to visit a patient and then report back, she wrestled with how to maintain confidentiality and healthy boundaries with both individuals. Though this boundary work was hard, she recognized that these lessons would aid her in congregational ministry. She also recognized the need for colleagues in ministry who could be resources to her as she wrestled with some of the pain and suffering she encountered. As chaplains we often expe-rience some of the more painful aspects of life and engage suffering on a daily basis. If we are to remain grounded and connected to our chaplaincy work, we need to create healthy boundaries and strong collaborative relationships that can nurture our soul.

QUESTIONS FOR REFLECTION

1. When you first came into this work, what were your fears and anxieties? What "bumps" did you experience, and how would you consider sharing those with a new and anxious student? (I would advise not sharing any stories that would increase their anxiety.)
2. When do you tend to want "to fix" someone? Are there themes from your own life that, if triggered, cause you to turn into a "hope dealer"? How will you help students recognize their "fix-it" tendencies and discern what their triggers may be?
3. What practices or people sustain you in the midst of your work? Are you able to set good boundaries in your ministry? How can you share these practices with your students?

SUGGESTED READINGS

DiAngelo, Robin. *White Fragility: Why It's so Hard for White People to Talk about Racism.* Boston: Beacon, 2018.
Ellison, Gregory, II. *Fearless Dialogues: A New Movement for Justice.* Louisville, KY: Westminster John Knox Press, 2017.
Fukuyama, Mary, and Todd Sevig. "Cultural Diversity in Pastoral Care." *Journal of Health Care Chaplaincy* 13, no. 2 (February 2004): 25–42.
Sanders, Cody, and Angela Yarber. *Microaggressions in Ministry: Confronting the Hidden Violence of Everyday Church.* Louisville, KY: Westminster John Knox Press, 2015.

Chapter Seventeen

Mentoring in Online Media

Axel Schoeber

Here in the Olympic City of Vancouver (British Columbia) is a restaurant where patrons eat their entire meal in the dark. Other major world cities also offer this experience in blind dining. The servers are visually impaired or entirely blind, and patrons enter their world. You cannot use light-emitting devices, including cellular phones. I imagine that darkness at least covers up spills and messes produced by the fact that I cannot see. However, the restaurant aims at a higher purpose: "Without the sense of sight, the senses of touch, taste, hearing and smell are intensified, allowing a new perception of reality."[1]

When we mentor through online media, we often move into similarly unfamiliar territory. It is highly likely that you have been selected to mentor an intern in a supervised field placement in ministry *because* you have shown skill in shaping others in the demanding, ever-shifting roles into which ministry practitioners must grow. So, congratulations are in order. But here is the rub: because you have demonstrated skill in face-to-face (f2f) ministry work and (probably) in f2f shaping and mentoring of novice ministry practitioners, you may be reluctant to transfer your skills to the online mode. Like fine dining in the dark, you will be unable to rely on some of the cues you depend upon heavily to gauge reactions that need processing. I am assuming that some of your mentoring will take place in purely verbal online settings such as e-mail, text, and chat groups. You cannot read the eyes or body language or watch facial inflections. You may be tempted to believe, therefore, that a mentoring experience that relies on the digital world is subpar or inadequate. It need not be. You will deploy other means of interaction, and you can sharpen your capacity to rely on them to provide a deepening experience for your intern. You, too, can enjoy fine dining in the dark.

I write out of my experience of teaching supervised ministry as an online course with no f2f components. I did so for eight years before returning to pastoral work. My first impressions of student growth and growth areas were formed by digital text. Yet students consistently reported that the course was highly personal and formative. It is possible to mentor well online.

Most of us involved in theological education know that online delivery of courses and other formative experiences will increase in the days ahead. One key benefit is increasing accessibility to such education for people whose circumstances make it difficult to move to a brick-and-mortar seminary campus. Soon a time will come when I do not need to encourage people that they can work effectively online. Digital natives will be doing the mentoring. Their challenge, if one exists, may be to learn the f2f components of ministry and mentoring. With a conscious awareness of "built-in obsolescence" for my words, I write for the current generation of mentors who have demonstrated effective f2f capacities and are uncertain whether they can transfer them sufficiently to an online environment. Do you really want to expend the energy to savor blind dining? I want to suggest that you can and, given technological change, we must.

Despite the title of this chapter, I will not suggest specific vehicles for use in online mentoring. I avoid this task for two reasons. First, each mentoring relationship is unique. In recent years, the number of online platforms that supplement digital text with video contact has increased—whether used to deliver formal course work in some cases, or to provide personal contact such as you are likely to engage in. You probably should incorporate them into your planned interactions. However, what you need will depend upon the interns' and your own personal circumstances. Different time zones, the platforms available in technology you both already have access to, the cost in money of accessing a new platform or in time of learning how to use it, and the limitations on internet use in both of your locations all could affect your decision on what works best. I suggest you practice discretion. You will assist your intern to grow in ministry capacity, not to develop brand loyalty to a certain platform. So, relax in the freedom to be practical and choose what is best for this relationship.

The second reason I will not evaluate current delivery vehicles is that the proliferation and development of these platforms is so rapid. If I gave my best assessments and recommendations today, they probably would be outdated by the time this book is published. I do not wish my words to become obsolete quite that fast.

HOW TO GROW AS AN ONLINE MENTOR

I begin with a qualification: I will rely on fellow contributors to this book to give further input regarding steps you can take to help your intern grow capacities in various facets of ministry life. Much of it can be applied, with creativity, to an online relationship. For example, if you cannot be present to witness sermon delivery, a combination of watching or listening to the message online and reviewing the feedback of several selected people who were present provides quite comprehensive input. Forms for such feedback usually can be obtained from the intern's seminary and then forwarded to the intern to distribute. You might need to coach the student on the variety of people to include among the reviewers.

I will focus on specific online points of growth.

First, let me encourage you to keep growing as a person. You will need to practice interpersonal skills at a high level to mentor online. It is important, for example, to keep growing in your capacity to provide effective, honest feedback in a variety of settings. The Apostle Paul spoke simply of "speaking the truth in love" (Ephesians 4:15). It is beguilingly easy to say those words; it is much harder to practice them. So often, truth or love seem to prevail, and we find it difficult to keep them together. You should value every setting in which you can deepen this skill. For when you are doing so in digital text or, even, through a video contact, you want to use your best ability as a means of gauging the interactions in this setting. The better you learn to communicate with wisdom, the more your effectiveness in life and ministry will increase in all areas. So, learning to mentor online provides a beneficial feedback loop for your whole life. Speaking the truth in love is only one example of personal growth that will benefit your online mentoring. Keep growing as a person.

A second part of personal growth that I should emphasize for online mentoring is listening. Ministry practitioners generally are adept at finding words to deploy for ministry's sake. It is a critical skill. (By the way, careful response to digital texts can sharpen an intern's capacity to work with words in all settings. You can correct inaccurate, demeaning, hostile, or deceptive words, and the student will grow significantly.) Some folk in ministry, however, are not strong listeners. To mentor online, you will have to keep sharpening this skill; it is crucial to your success. It is the capacity that helps you overcome the lack of physical interaction; it allows you to enjoy the "food you cannot see."

As you pay attention to your intern, notice what I call "absence." On two occasions, I observed students in my online courses start off with prolific and eager posting, then tail off noticeably part way through. In both cases I picked up the phone to have a live conversation and found out that a personal reaction to something in the course had thrown them off track. They had lost momentum. In both cases, they subsequently acknowledged that the conversation (which can now be conducted through a variety of platforms) was crucial to recovering their momentum. One student received a letter grade of A; the other, an A-. (The course was another one, not supervised ministry, for which I prefer to give no grade.) I probably would have noticed their struggle a little earlier in the course if it had been f2f. However, by paying attention to absence I contacted them, and they regained their momentum. So, I encourage you to watch for silence, absence, or loss of momentum in your intern. Follow up if you notice these dynamics.

Use your listening skills in online interactions, too. Pay very close attention, for example, to the choice of words in digital text communications or to hesitations in video chats. Ask about an unusual word. It could indicate more about a situation than so far has become apparent. Could it indicate the intern evading responsibility for his part in a relational misstep? Could he have missed the key opportunity to minister in a tricky situation? Ask tentatively; you could be wrong. But be bold enough to ask. With good listening skills applied in this fashion, you could surprise yourself (and your intern) at the depths you are reaching without being physically present to one another.

Gratefully I remember a student who quietly told me on a phone call: "You are the only person in the world, besides my wife, who knows about this issue for me." He is a very effective pastor, but he would not have lasted in the role without dealing with his own expectations of himself. He also told me, "My wife is so grateful that you and I are talking about this challenge." It was an online mentoring situation that led to deep transformation. The depth of the resolution in this instance was exceptional; it was not exceptional, however, in that online interaction with my students frequently led to transformation. So, be encouraged—and sharpen, sharpen, sharpen your listening skills so that they can be deployed in online settings. You will rejoice at the outcome.

Third, you need not feel confined to the primary medium in which you communicate with your intern. I have mentioned the use of a telephone call already. You have a variety of other ways you can connect. When you sense the need, contact the intern. Do not wait for her to make a request. Be like the shepherd who leaves the ninety-nine sheep to seek the one that was lost. If you discover the intern faltering in some fashion, you could well help her clarify an issue that will be part of equipping her for longevity and effectiveness in ministry. I expect, like the shepherd, you will experience much joy on those occasions (Luke 15:3–6). I have heard some folk express concern that it is intrusive to "pursue" someone outside the agreed upon medium. You will find, I believe—if you do not assume something is wrong but approach the intern out of care for her well-being—that instead the intern will be grateful for the connection. You both, of course, will rejoice in any opportunities you may have to meet physically in one place—whether or not you have an issue to address.

Fourth, I suggest you spend enough time learning to use your digital platform and hardware well. You do not want your online interactions disrupted by poorly functioning tools. Of course, you may find that the tools are not suitable for your situation. Then, investigate what will work effectively. However, it is wise to make sure that you are using the platform and/or hardware properly first, before you go to that extra work. On the other hand, here is a warning for some (not all): I would recommend that you monitor the time you spend on these tools so that you do not overdo it. A fascination with technology could detract from the real objective: to mentor well.

CONCLUSION

You may be aware that Ludwig van Beethoven (who really was great even if he did not appear on bubble gum cards, the standard applied by Lucy in the *Charlie Brown Christmas* special) grew increasingly deaf during his career as a composer. Toward the end he composed magnificent music though he could not hear it. Two factors contributed to his continued skill. First, he replaced hearing with touch: playing the piano key to feel its vibration and using that sensation to guide him in selecting the most appropriate notes. Second, he used his imagination to "hear" his compositions, allowing remembered experience to help him create new music. Both strategies have relevance for mentoring online.

I encourage you to use whatever tools you can to replace the input that you would derive from being physically present with your intern. I also encourage you to use your "ministry imagination" to anticipate the moments the intern may be finding himself in. Remember your own reactions when you first were in parallel situations. Remember, too, what you are learning about the ways in which the intern responds to new challenges, both strengths and weaknesses. By deploying your imagination and your skills in improvising, you can assist the intern—online—to create an impressive symphony with his ministry life. You will rejoice, even if the intern gets the credit.

QUESTIONS FOR REFLECTION

1. How can you enhance your listening skills for the sake of life, ministry, and your intern?
2. In what ways can you practice improvisation in your online mentoring relationship?
3. How much time do you spend on the technical side of online mentoring, working with the tools? Do you ensure that the relational side remains the priority?

4. What platforms and hardware do you find most helpful right now?

5. Are you ensuring that you have enough f2f ministry contact so that you can rejoice in the creativity of online mentoring rather than feel wearied by it? (This final question arises from my own experience. True confession: because I spent more than eight years teaching and mentoring almost entirely online, I have become somewhat "digitally avoidant." I find myself less than enthusiastic about doing my ministry through e-mail and other online means, though I still do it. I am very grateful that most of my interactions are now f2f.)

SUGGESTED READINGS

Blodgett, Barbara J. *Becoming the Pastor You Hope to Be: Four Practices for Improving Ministry*. Herndon, VA: Alban, 2011.

Cahalan, Kathleen A. *Introducing the Practice of Ministry*. Collegeville, MN: Liturgical Press, 2010.

Kincaid, William B. *Finding Voice: How Theological Field Education Shapes Pastoral Identity*. Eugene, OR: Wipf & Stock, 2012.

Schoeber, Axel. "Making Space for Online Students to Create Relevancy from Course Content for Their Contexts." *Reflective Practice*, 36 (2016): 63–76, http://journals.sfu.ca/rpfs/index.php/rpfs/article/view/425/412.

———. "Shaped Digitally: Supervised Ministry in Online Environments." *Theological Education* 50, no. 2 (2017): 169–82, https://www.ats.edu/uploads/resources/publicationspresentations/theological-education/2017-theological-education-v50-n2.pdf.

Chapter Eighteen

The Congregation as Mentor

Matthew Floding

THE CHURCH MENTORS

Do you promise
to instruct this child
in the truth of God's word,
in the way of salvation through Jesus Christ;
to pray for this child, to teach this child to pray;
and to train this one in Christ's way by your example,
through worship, and
in the nurture of the church?
We do, and we ask God to help us. [1]

I think my church tried to keep faith with its baptismal promises. I remember Mrs. Nelson, in my second grade Sunday School class, teaching us about God who calls all Christians to ministry through the story of Samuel's call. I remember vividly the passion with which our Scout leader, Mr. Peterson, celebrated the Creator God at campfires and instilled in us a creation care ethic: "Pack it in, pack it out boys. Leave only footprints!" Later I received sage advice from elders as I discerned my call to ordained ministry during college. In field education the host church, by extension, honored those baptismal promises in its patient participation in my formation. As a newly minted clergy, the church continued to be faithful in my ministerial formation. The church's members, the local funeral director, and a neighboring Presbyterian minister guided me through my first funeral two weeks after being installed. Sometime later, a wise elder drew me aside and counseled me to value people and process as much as the wonderful program goals I was pushing. On and on it goes.

When you reflect on your formation, do you see God's people at work?

Recall how many times you have stood before God and the parent(s) of a little one being baptized and made promises like those above. Think of it: your pastoral intern was once the precious child for whom a congregation made promises. Your role is a significant part of the fulfillment of those promises. But not alone.

In the same way that it is unrealistic to expect that seminary students can be educated for ministerial service simply by going to classes, it would also be unfair to think that a pastor or ministerial leader is the only person who should mentor an intern in a broad range of ministerial activities. In fact, it would be denying teachings about the nature of the church. For example, Paul writes in 1 Corinthians 12:4–7,

> Now there are varieties of gifts, but the same Spirit; and there are varieties of services, but the same Lord; and there are varieties of activities, but it is the same God who activates them all in everyone. To each is given the manifestation of the Spirit for the common good.

Theological education is best done by the whole church—not just the ordained clergy and professors. Imagine a team of lay persons committed to mentoring your seminary student by engaging in intentional practices of ministerial reflection and vocational discernment. The theological field education program you collaborate with strongly encourages this. The seminary or divinity school may call it a lay mentoring team or a lay committee.

WHAT DOES IT LOOK LIKE?

Your congregation or other ministerial setting is providing a gift of inestimable worth to a seminary student: the place to practice ministry and spaces to reflect on that practice with you and members or participants in your context.

Laurent Parks Daloz et al. introduced two helpful concepts related to mentoring in their book *Common Fire: Leading Lives of Commitment in a Complex World.*[2] The first is the *hospitable space* that welcomes the learning-serving participation of your seminary student in all aspects of the congregation's or nonprofit's ministry. This is critical to the formation of a person's ministerial identity. Try this thought experiment. Most congregations value preaching. Imagine that your seminary intern only is allowed to preach in her senior year, once per semester. This was the policy of one congregation. How does this policy help this soon-to-be-minister develop what most believe to be an important ministry competency? (Sorry for the rhetorical question.)

In our "Litany of Beginnings" at Duke Divinity School (for use in congregational settings), we try to make this notion of hospitable space explicit. Here's a portion of our recommended litany.

Ministerial intern: I have come to serve and learn with this congregation.

Chair of lay mentoring team: We have been called as a congregation to be for (student's name) a teaching and learning community.

People: We welcome you into our community, (student's name), as God's representative. Our homes, our hospitals and nursing homes, our classrooms and programs, our sanctuary, our lives, are all open to you.

The second concept is *threshold persons*. These are trustworthy and transformational relationships with significant persons. It may be helpful to think of it this way. Your intern is on the threshold of discovery, but he needs a guide to show the way, to support him in his efforts, and to reflect on his experience in order to learn and return to the activity with increased confidence and competency. You probably can name half a dozen persons easily from your context who could be that kind of person for your student.

Daloz and his colleagues discovered that a capacity for connection, for reflective, creative, strategic, and committed engagement with complex issues is nurtured in environments that share these two qualities. If this is so, seminary and divinity school students who certainly will face complexity, uncertainty, and ambiguity in their ministry will benefit by participation in these kinds of spaces and with these kinds of persons.

You can form a team of these persons. Consider carefully who would best complement you in this mentoring opportunity. Can your seminarian read a balance sheet? No problem. Invite a CPA to share his knowledge and skills with your student. Would he like to grow in caregiving skills? Wonderful. You can provide pastoral care opportunities and mentor your student and extend that by inviting a therapist to serve on the mentoring team. She can explore additional dimensions of caregiving with your student. Teaching? Invite the middle-school master teacher to team teach with your student. You get the idea. By populating your mentoring team with committed members from your ministerial setting, your student experiences the "varieties of services, but the same Lord."

For the persons you recruit, this could be one of the most deeply satisfying ministry commitments they have ever made. It also underscores an important value that you've learned as a ministerial leader. Do not go it alone. Do not try to be a hero. To this point Samuel Wells writes:

Of those sixty-four references to saints in the New Testament, every one is in the plural. Saints are never alone. They assume, demand, require community— a special kind of community, the communion of saints. Heroes have learned to depend on themselves; saints learn to depend on God and the community of faith. [3]

Your student has the opportunity to experience the communion of saints. This, in turn, can encourage her to be non-defensive as a ministerial leader and empower her to lean into the "varieties of gifts, but the same Spirit."

STUDENTS REPORT

Students complete evaluations at the end of their field education experience. In ours, they evaluate self, supervisor-mentor, and site. Related to the site are a series of numerically scored questions such as

- This community helped bring clarity to my call, gifts, and pastoral identity.
- This community is a "teaching community" where my competencies were cultivated.

Some speak directly to the role of the lay mentoring team. [4]

- Members of the lay mentoring team took an interest in what I hoped to practice and learn about ministry.

Then there is space for a personal statement. Here are five.

My Lay Mentoring Team was very encouraging of me throughout the summer. Each were intentional about asking questions, sharing affirmations, and suggesting areas for growth. This went a long way in making me feel supported in my ministry. The entire congregation was very hospitable. From the first day to the last, they made me feel like part of their church family by including me in their lives, inviting me to dinner or other events, and sharing with me their joys and struggles. If the congregation had told me they had been helping form interns for 50 years, I would have believed it; that's how second-nature it is for them to welcome in strangers, love them well, and form them for Christian service. It is absolutely necessary that this community continue to be a place where students are formed for ministry.

I found the corporate environment of this non-profit to be wonderfully educational. This context allowed me to reconsider my own vision of what church administration and finances should look like. I loved getting to learn more about publishing, distribution, marketing, writing, editing, pastoral care, and everything in between. I learned more about compassion and pastoral care here than I have ever learned inside the walls of a church. This non-profit is an incredible place filled with beautiful, highly educated, brilliant, and caring people.

I have so loved this community! They are extremely active and committed to serving their community in the name of Jesus. My critique of them is also one of their greatest strengths: they are very capable on their own. I sometimes learned of ministry opportunities after the congregation had already completed the tasks. This seems like a good problem to have! I think they had to slow down to make space for me to practice! James was especially helpful in navigating the organizational side of ministry and learning how to manage or work with it. They are a wonderful and supportive bunch, they just move very quickly!

All four Mentoring Team members were kind, hospitable, welcoming and generous. I took note and was blessed to see lay leadership modeled so well. I felt as though each walked alongside me, and my ministry competencies were sharpened and nurtured, especially teaching. I experienced the joy of a great teacher. No wonder she's been doing it for more than twenty years!

I loved being placed in this agency. This agency provides multidimensional and nuanced perspectives of ministry and the praxis of ministry outside of four walls. This placement will open the eyes of Divinity students, if they allow it, to injustice and oppression right in our backyard. It will challenge students to reconsider what "welcoming the neighbor" actually looks like in the field. The staff taught and modeled so many skills that engaged a variety of publics theologically. I will be a better advocate for it. I highly recommend this placement for future students.

As you read these, you can sense the character of these ministries. Hospitable spaces welcome a student to formational possibilities. Threshold persons stand ready to make experiences of all kinds accessible, to coach, and to cheer their student on. Your student will experience the communion of saints forming them for ministry. You can make it so in your ministerial context.

QUESTIONS FOR REFLECTION

1. Recall with joy and gratitude how the people of God have participated in your ministerial formation.
2. With that group of persons in mind, who in your context could serve your student as those did for you?
3. How might you help your congregation or nonprofit embrace its teaching community role as a calling from God?

SUGGESTED READINGS

Floding, Matthew. "Fostering a Mentoring Environment." In *Reflective Practice: Formation and Supervision in Ministry*, 272–81.

Howell, Sarah S. "Kingdom Mentoring." In *Mentoring for Ministry: The Grace of Growing Pastors*, edited by Craig T. Kocher, Jason Byasee, and James C. Howell. Eugene, OR: Wipf and Stock, 2017.

Kincaid, William. "Finding Your Place in the System." In *Finding Voice: How Theological Field Education Shapes Pastoral Identity*. Eugene, OR: Wipf and Stock, 2012.

Mason, George. *Preparing the Pastors We Need: Reclaiming the Congregation's Role in Training Clergy*. Lanham, MD: Rowman & Littlefield, 2012.

Chapter Nineteen

Mentoring beyond Seminary

Allison St. Louis

"They didn't teach us that in seminary!"

It's a common refrain, one that has been—or will be—uttered by most seminary graduates. It is both a reminder that seminary curricula offer limited educational and formational experiences and that seminarians are not always ready to learn from all that is offered. As a result, experienced, competent mentors can be a welcome gift to novice ministers.

Although seminary graduates usually continue to develop competence in the practical tasks of ministry, via supervised practice and/or by taking advantage of the wealth of continuing education offerings, many novice ministers report that intra- and/or interpersonal issues bring them to the edge of their competency and comfort zone. Over the past nine years, my ministry as a field educator and director of a transition into ministry program has included numerous discussions with seminarians, lay leaders, and newly ordained graduates about such issues. The following list, although not exhaustive, is intended to highlight some common challenges and to offer a few suggestions for mentors who are helping novice ministers to navigate these issues.

CENTERING LIVES AND MINISTRIES ON GOD

Although our mentees recognize that people of faith are called to model a spiritually grounded approach to life, they often find themselves mirroring the frenetic, unsettled lives of many in our society. Overscheduled living leaves little time for self- and/or theological reflection. Not surprising, a common complaint from mentees is their frustration at not being able to develop a life-giving rhythm of regular, private devotions, personal retreats, and Bible study. To their dismay, they often confine reading the Bible to sermon preparation. On the other hand, mentees who create space for private prayer sometimes feel guilty for not spending that time in ministry. Others become resentful when their personal prayer time is interrupted repeatedly by "nonemergency emergencies." Those who are not interrupted by external demands are distracted by intrusive thoughts concerning items on their to-do list. However, doing and being need not be enemies: doing with God that springs from being with God can bear much life-giving fruit. On the other hand, doing that is not grounded in our relationship with God and knowledge of ourselves, including the limits that are part of being an embodied self, can become chaotic, reactive, or meaningless.

By modeling spiritually grounded living (e.g., attending to their relationship with God by engaging in regular Bible study, practicing weekly Sabbath, going on annual retreats); being willing to discuss the practices, challenges, and rewards of tending to their relationship with God; and providing support, guidance and feedback as mentees experiment with finding the spiritual practices that work best for them, given their disposition and context, mentors can help novice ministers to cultivate the art of God-centered living.

EMBRACING BELOVEDNESS

Some mentees live with the lingering effects of negative messages about self and/or God from their families of origin, religious denominations, or societal institutions. For instance, some live with the anxiety of not feeling "worthy" of God's love. Spending time alone with God can provoke even more anxiety, and ministry can become an attempt to appease God's anger, mitigate God's retribution, and earn God's love. Coupled with the complex and unrelenting demands of ministry, this belief system can lead to behaviors that give rise to resentment, isolation, and burnout.

By accepting mentees where they are, listening deeply to their fears, joys, and aspirations, avoiding the temptation to mold them into the mentor's image, committing to pray for them regularly, and challenging them to grow into the self that God has created them to be, supervisor-mentors who have embraced their own belovedness can assist their mentees with doing the same.

COUNTERING TEMPTATIONS

Becoming grounded in a relationship with God in which they embrace with heart and mind that God's love for them is unconditional and irrevocable nurtures our mentees' sense of well-being. It also helps them to accept their gifts and limitations. Further, embracing their belovedness can free them from the bondage of defining their worth as ministers and as human beings by their ability to meet the limitless demands of ministry. These are important foundational elements as mentees will encounter manifold temptations to center their lives and ministries on productivity, power, and prestige/popularity gone awry (Matthew 4:1–11; Luke 4:1–13).

For instance, the natural desire to be liked easily can become the deciding factor in a mentee's ministerial decisions. The actions that arise from such decisions are neither realistic nor respectful of the mentee. They also can develop into a habit of avoiding or provoking conflict, misusing social media, harboring prejudices toward those on the margins, and/or comparing themselves to and competing with their peers. To compound matters, some mentees are susceptible to accepting denominational definitions of success, definitions that simply mirror secular versions of success. As one denominational leader observed, "Isn't it funny how God hardly ever seems to call pastors to move from a higher paying position in a large church to a less well-paying position in a small church?"[1]

By working with mentees to clarify their core values, discern how God is calling them to employ their unique gifts and skills, and build a support system of faithful, committed spiritual leaders, supervisor-mentors can help novice ministers navigate political, social, and denominational pressures to define success in terms other than faithfulness to God's call. For instance, supervisor-mentors can use various online tools (e.g., https://www.valuescentre.com/our-products/products-individuals/personal-value-sassessment-pva) to assist their mentees in thinking through what they value, what motivates them, and to use that increased self-knowledge to discern the kind of ministry to which they may be well-suited.

NAVIGATING BOUNDARY CHALLENGES

Developing firm but flexible boundaries is an important part of dealing with the temptations just mentioned. Spiritual leaders, as well as those they serve, constantly are faced with challenges to their limits of time, energy, and other resources. The parishioner who wonders aloud why the clergy person went to the stewardship committee meeting but not to his Bible study session, the organist who refuses to play a particular hymn (or who protests by playing it like a dirge), and the parent who wants to use a church event as day care for his child all are examples of boundary challenges. These individuals engage in "overstepping" behaviors (e.g., an organist is not hired to play only those hymns that he likes).

Such actions not only disregard the spiritual leader's role and responsibilities to the larger community (e.g., selecting hymns based on the readings from scripture and the needs of the community, not solely on personal preference), they also dismiss the purpose of, as well as the resources that are available for, a particular event (e.g., a desire to use a church event simply as day care, whether or not day care is provided, and not for the purpose for which it was designed). Perhaps the one that virtually all mentees face is the disgruntled parishioner who complains to the mentee (who is usually the new, junior pastor/assistant priest) about the senior pastor/priest. These experiences can be a significant source of stress to our mentees. Those who are unsure of themselves or of how to set limits may react by engaging in overly flexible or overly inflexible behaviors. For instance, a mentee once stated that she thought she was "supposed to be available 24/7"[2] to everyone in her community. In contrast, another mentee refused to go to her parish to help the senior clergy on September 11, 2001, because that was her "day off."[3]

By allowing mentees to observe and learn from those who have developed firm but flexible boundaries, who share and reflect on their as well as their mentees' past, current, and anticipated future boundary challenges, and who reflect on case studies with mentees in peer groups, mentors can help their mentees gain insight and devise strategies for dealing with boundary issues. For instance, a mentor can talk with her mentees about how she learned to deal with repeated, late night, "nonemergency" phone calls from a member of her community, including the process of gently and firmly sharing with that individual her understanding of an emergency and guiding that individual in making use of appropriate sources of support in the wider community (e.g., therapist, spiritual director).

READING COMMUNITIES

In their enthusiasm and eagerness to serve God and God's people, some mentees rush headlong into making major changes shortly after arriving in their communities, particularly if they are the primary spiritual leader. Those who recognize and appreciate that they have entered an existing system, one that likely will be there after they leave, can use their entry into the system as an opportunity to be curious. Showing interest in the members of the community, developing relationships with key leaders as well as those on the margins and those in between, and asking questions in an effort to understand the who, what, when, where, how, and why of the system's historical and current functioning are all important aspects of entering a system.

By encouraging and challenging mentees to exercise patience and foresight as they engage the work of building a strong, relational foundation with the members of their community and by helping them to discern how and when to implement significant changes in the system, supervisor-mentors can provide invaluable guidance and coaching to novice ministers. For instance, supervisor-mentors can encourage mentees to devote time to developing one-to-one relationships with as many members of the community as possible, to researching the history of the community, and to creating a congregational genogram aimed at understanding the emotional functioning of the community (e.g., lay-clergy relationships, how the community functions under stress, how it relates to the surrounding community). This groundwork can help the mentee gain an understanding of that unique community and build strong relationships with its members before introducing significant changes.

CLARIFYING EXPECTATIONS

From particular financial or personnel challenges facing the community that were not shared or inquired about during the interview process to the expectations that spiritual leaders have of themselves, unspoken and unmet expectations can result in otherwise avoidable conflict. Clarifying expectations is vital to preempting unnecessary conflict, setting priorities, and managing time. To that end, novice ministers who are serving with senior priests and governing bodies may need to learn the art of asking gentle, clarifying questions.

Mentors can help mentees cultivate the art of clarifying expectations and use their time in inner-directed and responsive, rather than outer-directed and reactive, ways by:

- offering wisdom to mentees as they prepare for interviews;
- helping them to create a list of interview questions, including ones related to the supervisor's and community's expectations of the new minister;
- reviewing their résumés and conducting mock interviews, if requested;
- guiding mentees on how to address sensitive issues related to compensation, vacation, and sabbatical time;
- encouraging them regularly to assess how their use of time reflects their core values, their short- and long-term ministry goals, and their vision for their ongoing life with God.

GROWING A SELF

A common mistake that novice ministers make is neglecting self and/or family in an effort to be "all things to all people." Pressure from self or others to be the expert can lead to difficulty with admitting that they do not know the answer to a question. Nonetheless, God's call to serve as spiritual leaders, whether lay or ordained, brings us face-to-face with our limitations. The mystery of God and God's creation is such that, even after a lifetime of learning and growth, the vast expanse of our inner and outer worlds will remain uncharted.

Mentors can help novice ministers to cooperate with God in growing them up in ways that respect their uniqueness and integrity by:

- supporting their mentees' efforts to address the physical, emotional, spiritual, social, and financial needs that are part of being an embodied self;
- challenging them to learn about how they function, as well as how they can grow, during times of conflict;
- helping them to accept that they do not know everything;
- assisting them with discerning what can and ought to be known, and what cannot be known—or known only in part—during this earthly lifetime;
- encouraging them to engage in lifelong learning while also living in the tension of not knowing as much as they think they "should."

Given the varied challenges that novice ministers face, it is highly unlikely that one mentor will be able to meet all of a mentee's needs. Novice ministers may benefit from having at least two or three mentors who can offer their wisdom and insights, guidance, and support in specific areas of their ministry. Likewise, mentors may benefit from supporting one another in this invaluable ministry. Those who choose to expand and deepen their mentoring skills via a peer group may find it helpful to explore three questions and/or ones that they evoke:

1. What qualities and skills do you appreciate in a mentor?
2. What are some of the current challenges confronting most novice ministers?
3. How might we support our mentees in their desire to be faithful to God's call?

SUGGESTED READINGS

Friedman, Edwin H. *A Failure of Nerve: Leadership in the Age of the Quick Fix*. New York: Seabury, 2007.

McCreath, Amy. "The Ministry of Mentoring in the 21st Century Church." In *Resources for American Christianity*, http://www.resourcingchristianity.org.

Percy, Martin P., Ian S. Markham, Emma Percy, and Francesca Po, eds. *The Study of Ministry: A Comprehensive Survey of Theory and Best Practice*. London: Society for Promoting Christian Knowledge, 2019.

Scazzero, Peter. *The Emotionally Healthy Leader: How Transforming Your Inner Life Will Deeply Transform Your Church, Team, and the World*. Grand Rapids, MI: Zondervan, 2015.

Thompson, Dean K., and Cameron D. Murchison, eds. *Mentoring: Biblical, Theological and Practical Perspectives*. Grand Rapids, MI: Eerdmans, 2018.

III

Mentoring for Leadership Formation

Chapter Twenty

Mentoring for Courageous Leadership

William B. Kincaid

It takes courage to sit across from someone, to listen closely, to navigate the unfolding of a relationship, and to lean into an uncertain future together. It takes courage to be open to hearing new truth, especially when it is about ourselves, and sometimes even more courage to speak truth to another person. To be present to one another involves courage.

And I'm not even talking about mentoring and supervising yet. I'm just describing the level of courage required for any meaningful encounter and relationship between two people.

I start there to remind us of some of the dynamics at play when we sit with another person. I want first to situate our supervisory conversations in that context. Before the first report on an event in ministry, before the first theological reflection, before the first spark of pastoral imagination gets kindled, two people are sitting together. Two people are gazing upon the glory of God and the vulnerabilities of being human in the other. Two people are assessing each other and plotting their next move in the conversation and the relationship. And all of that involves courage. Lots of courage.

I know I haven't always brought that kind of fierce presence to every conversation, including supervisory sessions, but I approach this chapter with the assumption that courage breeds courage. We aren't likely to nurture courageous leadership in others if we blink, hedge, or otherwise hold back some part of ourselves. Though some situations and events evoke courage in us, courage often is cultivated while observing and experiencing it in others. Just as the therapist-client relationship can spill its honesty and clarity into every other relationship of which we are part, so the mentor-mentee relationship becomes a crucible in which courage is recognized, nurtured, claimed, and embodied. In other words, we will only foster courage in our students and mentees when we bring courage to supervisory conversations.

REFLECTIONS ON MY MENTORS IN MINISTRY

My mentoring impulses largely come from my own mentors. I assume that is true for most of us. Whatever supervisory approach or theory my mentors might have been using at the time, nothing registered more clearly than when I realized that a supervisor-mentor really was risking something of herself in the session. Those occasions when the supervisor-mentor clearly gave herself over to the moment and over to my formation startled and even scared me, but a larger vocation emerged in those moments, one that only can be answered with courage.

It takes nerve and time to discern the character and possibilities of such a vocation. The most courageous supervisors are the patient ones. They have no need to overwhelm, embarrass, or accelerate the process to satisfy their own egos or position. Rather, they help students metabolize the inspiring and the terrifying so that they can grow accustomed to holding the two in creative tension.

On the other hand, supervisor-mentors who made too little of supervision and mentoring or too much of themselves as supervisor-mentors often left me wondering what, if anything, was at stake. Of course, it humbles me greatly to confront the certainty that trivializing and self-aggrandizing occurred in my supervisory work, but I would be displaying a harmful cowardice to look back at some of those sessions and see anything else. Sometimes confessing the lack of courage in one season can inspire courage in a new season.

WHAT CONSTITUTES RISK IN SUPERVISION?

We can deceive ourselves when we think about what we are risking as supervisor-mentors. For example, supervisor-mentors will calibrate the sharing of personal stories at different registers depending on their own views toward such sharing, as well as on particular students and circumstances. My students tell me they want more stories from my pastoral ministry than I am inclined to share. They are affirming that they hear pastoral wisdom in these stories, I suppose, but much of it comes from pastoral clumsiness and comical church situations. That's what they really enjoy.

It took years for me to be honest enough with myself to acknowledge that I sometimes told stories to cause both the mentee and myself to look away from the real conversation or perhaps to keep us from ever finding it in the first place. Stories can take us to deep places that expose the rawness of life and the exhilarating nature of hope, but they also can divert our gaze and ensure that we avoid any challenging and life-giving depth.

The poet William Stafford said, "Armor is fine, but it keeps you from knowing what the weather feels like."[1] How a supervisor-mentor wears and sets aside the armor is a measure of the presence and currency of courage in the supervisory encounter. Doing so also holds up a mirror for mentees as they begin to understand their own armor, become increasingly aware of the challenges it presents, and learn how and when to set it aside for authentic ministry.

We all wear armor of some kind. Its material may come from the need to be liked by parishioners and well regarded by colleagues and mentees, or from personal and professional wounds whose scab is knocked off easily, or from compensating for a crisis of faith while continuing to perform pastoral roles week after week. And as we all know but do not quickly appreciate or admit, we can wear some form of armor for years without even realizing it.

We foster courage as supervisor-mentors when our own mentees trust that we know what the weather feels like. That involves more than opening an app or consulting a local weather source. We know what the weather feels like because we make ourselves present and vulnerable to its warm sun and its cold wind. We know the joy and heartache of a place and of a particular faith community because we have removed the armor for the sake of genuine presence and engagement.

Students will lean into conversations when they know that we have felt the loneliness of leadership decisions, the breathtaking vulnerability of the ICU, the inspiration of worship before a high and lifted-up God, and the daily vocation of easing human suffering and changing the unjust systems that caused it. Our supervision and mentoring fosters courage when mentees know that we know what the weather feels like and that we don't run for cover every time a storm starts brewing several states away. Even if initially it is unsettling, mentees trust mentors who drop their guardedness and talk honestly and hopefully about things as they really are.

THE FINAL EXPRESSION OF SUPERVISORY COURAGE

Perhaps the most difficult dimension of courageous mentoring is releasing the mentee, as well as the mentee releasing the mentor. Great leaders assist individuals and organizations in letting go so that they can embrace an emerging portion of the new creation. Courageous mentors do the same.

The time comes for the mentee to pursue her particular calling, even if that calling is very different from that of the mentor's and one that the mentor struggles to understand and bless. The moment arrives for the mentee to launch out on his own, even if the mentor wants a little more time to impart wisdom and warnings. And at its best, the relationship evolves over time into a collegial one, but all of this requires letting go. We humans don't do that easily, and we never do it apart from courage.

A CONVERSATION IN SEARCH OF COURAGE

The local seminary paired Jared[2] with me because of my familiarity with the congregation and the town where he was serving. That's not a bad reason to create a supervisory relationship, but we stumbled through nearly an entire year of supervision together. He was a master of divinity student in his mid-forties whose hometown in another state had elected him twice as district attorney. I was a relatively recent seminary graduate and with far fewer years of ministry experience than he had as a practicing attorney.

Over time, I came to recognize a troubling common thread in the sessions. It seemed to me that he was holding back. I didn't think he was engaging the process with any openness, seriousness, or anticipation. I resented that but felt reticent to challenge him for some reason.

The question, of course, is Why? Why didn't this work matter more to either of us?

Late in the year I asked him, "So are you just here for the credentials?" The question took him totally by surprise.

"What? No. I want to learn. I need to learn. I'm serious about this."

"But we've spent a whole year together, and I'm not sure we have much to show for it."

"Well," he started hesitantly, "I've been waiting on you. You're the supervisor. I'm new to this. I don't know what we are supposed to be doing here. Introspection and self-confrontation weren't part of law school."

At the very least, I had not communicated my expectation well enough that the student owns the responsibility for setting the agenda for supervisory sessions, but that wasn't all. I realized that I had made assumptions about Jared and our supervisory sessions that significantly undermined the experience. Perhaps worse than that, I recognized that I was a little intimidated by Jared and his professional accomplishments. Instead of calling on my training, playing to my strengths, trusting the process, and fulfilling my role, I let other factors cloud and complicate our relationship. Jared waited on me while I continued to assume at some level both that I couldn't possibly offer him anything of value and that, even if I could, he would not be interested.

My question about whether Jared was in seminary just for the credentialing exhibited a bit of courage, but Jared showed more courage when he called me on my own hesitance and lack of pressing. I share this story as a reminder of courage's power to open a conversation, regardless of who demonstrates it. The exchange completely changed the character, spirit, and depth of our supervisory experience. My only regret is that I didn't challenge

Jared sooner. Fortunately, instead of limping to the end of a year together, a breakthrough occurred that set the stage for a second year of supervision and mentoring. That year represents to this day one of the most honest, constructive, and fulfilling years of mentoring that I have experienced.

QUESTIONS FOR REFLECTION

The following questions may help supervisory colleagues reflect on their own practice and to approach supervisory sessions with self-awareness, clarity of purpose, and nerve.

1. As you prepare for a meeting with your supervisee, what do you need to set aside in advance of the time together in order to courageously mentor someone? You also should be prepared for moments in the session when something may surface that will need to be set aside in order to stay focused on fostering courage with your mentee. Just physically getting in the same room with an intern can stretch us and our calendars, but that is only the starting point. The real work is to be present in a credible way. And that takes courage.

2. What risk or discovery of your own can be the fuel for this session? Supervision can and should be an expression of the mentor's own faith and ministry adventure. Supervision that is dull and predictable doesn't benefit either the mentor or the mentee, and certainly not the church.

3. What conflict will help you go deeper in this supervisory session? Key breakthroughs occur when the conversation names an impediment and then works through it in interesting and helpful ways. Sometimes introducing a conflict into the conversation or the supervisory relationship leads to a surprisingly productive outcome. Doing so also helps students become more comfortable with the varieties and possibilities of conflict.

4. Do you know what it feels like when you reach for your armor and begin putting it back on during a supervisory session? Most of us do this in our relationships generally, especially during times of tension and anxiety. It's understandable that it would occur with a mentee as well. An awareness of what prompts this and what it feels like will benefit the supervisory process.

SUGGESTED READINGS

I offer a brief list of diverse genres that reflect the openness, honesty, and nerve involved in relationships in general and in ministry and mentoring in particular.

Ellison, Gregory C., II. *Fearless Dialogues: A New Movement for Justice*. Louisville, KY: Westminster John Knox Press, 2017.

Heyward, Carter. *Keep Your Courage: A Radical Christian Feminist Speaks*. New York: Church Publishing, 2011.

King, Martin Luther, Jr. *A Testament of Hope: The Essential Writings and Speeches*. New York: HarperOne, 2003.

Lee, Harper. *To Kill A Mockingbird*. New York: HarperCollins, 1960.

Olds, Sharon. *Stag's Leap: Poems*. New York: Knopf, 2012.

Robinson, Marilynne. *Gilead: A Novel*. New York: Farrar, Straus & Giroux, 2004.

Chapter Twenty-One

Mentoring the Preacher

Tracy Hartman

If you are looking for a step-by-step formula to mentor interns in the ministry of preaching, this chapter will disappoint you. One of the most significant challenges facing new preachers is finding and developing their own voices in the pulpit, and interns come to our ministry contexts at different places in this developmental process. They also approach preaching from a variety of points on a broad spectrum. At one end of the spectrum, many students approach preaching with fear and trembling. They are either highly anxious about public speaking, or they fear they are unworthy or ill-prepared to exegete and proclaim the Word of God. On the other end of the spectrum, some interns will come to us (over)confident that they know exactly what the church needs to hear and exactly which scriptures they can use in their fiery sermons to support their presuppositions. Most of our mentees will fall between these two extremes. Regardless of where they are in their journeys, all students will need mentoring in individualized ways that will help them find and develop their own unique voices and an appropriate level of confidence for preaching.

But there is good news: although no one-size-fits-all program exists for mentoring budding preachers, some broad principles can help us guide our students with wisdom, humor, and integrity.

WE ALL WALK A FINE LINE

As preachers, we all walk a fine line. On the one hand, going to the Word of God to hear, develop, and then release a message to the congregation is an awe-full responsibility, and one that we should indeed approach with fear and trembling. On the other hand, we can preach with confidence and the assurance that God will equip and empower us to do what we are called to do. Fearful preachers need the encouragement and affirmation that they do have a voice and message to share, and that they should do so with God-given confidence. For the most timid interns, we might need to start by having them read scripture and lead prayers (practicing with coaching mid-week) before they are ready to preach. Those who think they have it all figured out need to be reminded that they must approach the text with humility, willing to have their assumptions challenged and their presuppositions changed as they wrestle with God for a message for the people. As mentors, we must discern where our students need encouragement and where they need guidance and correction as they seek to walk the line.

INTERNS NEED PRACTICE, PRACTICE, PRACTICE

Kathleen Cahalan reminds us that it takes ten years to achieve competency in ministry, and this includes preaching.[1] The pastor of the church I attend has been with us for fifteen years. He served a sister church as an associate for several years before he came to our congregation, but this was his first senior pastor position. When he first arrived, his sermons were more than adequate, but it was clear that he was still working on finding and developing his own voice. Now, fifteen years later, he is a fine preacher. He knows and loves our congregation deeply, and he navigates the line of confidence and humility with intentionality.

One of the best things we can do for our interns is give them regular opportunities to preach, not just at Wednesday night prayer meeting or to the youth group on Sunday evening, but on Sunday mornings. We may need to help our members understand the role of a teaching congregation in mentoring young preachers and remind them that a variety of voices from the pulpit is healthy.

MODEL EXCELLENCE IN PREACHING

Observing and learning from excellent preachers helps interns develop their own unique voices for preaching. Time and time again, students report the importance of role models in their own growth as preachers. Set aside time to talk to your interns about your own process of sermon development. Share with them how you approach the text, what resources are helpful to you, how you decide on a sermon form, where you find your illustrations, and whether you take notes, an outline, or a full manuscript into worship with you. Help your interns connect with preachers of other genders, ethnicities, denominational affiliations, and theological persuasions so they can expand their own toolboxes for preaching.

ENCOURAGE INTERNS TO STRETCH THEMSELVES
IN NEW WAYS

Some students learn one specific method of sermon development and delivery in preaching class, whereas others learn a variety of sermon forms and delivery options. Either way, students may only have preached once or twice before they arrived in your church. As students continue to learn the art and craft of preaching in your setting, encourage them to try new things. Challenge a manuscript preacher to work from notes or even to preach without notes. Encourage those who speak impromptu and tend to chase rabbits to work from a solid outline to help them stay on track. Help students use different sermon forms to build their repertoires. This trial and error is an important part of skill building, but students must know that they are in a safe and nurturing environment for them to have the freedom to do this work.

Some students love to study and write sermons but don't like delivering them. Others enjoy public speaking but struggle with the discipline to study and prepare. Where are your students on this continuum, and how can you help them develop best practices from inception to delivery?

"NICE SERMON, PREACHER."

How many times have you heard this platitude from well-meaning congregants as you greet them in the narthex? As well-intentioned as these worshippers might be, such vague feedback is of little help to young preachers. Novice preachers need regular, specific feedback and coaching in order to help them grow. Some supervisors require interns to preach their sermons midweek, from the pulpit in the sanctuary, so that they have the opportunity to refine content and delivery before Sunday. Although interns report how nerve-racking it is to preach to one person, they are grateful for the feedback and the chance to improve before releasing the sermon to a larger audience.

Other interns will ask members of their support teams or another select group to provide written feedback on their sermons. This can be a valuable resource but one that should not be overused. Even in teaching congregations, we must balance asking congregants to be evaluators with their need to focus on worship—it is nearly impossible to do both at the same time.

Here is a sample form that our students use for congregational feedback:

Table 21.1. Sermon Feedback Form

Sermon Feedback Form

Preacher's Name:

Reviewer's Name:

Sermon Title:

Text:

Please check the appropriate box below according to the following scale:

1 = strongly agree, 2 = agree, 3 = neither agree/disagree, 4 = disagree, 5 = strongly disagree

Item	1	2	3	4	5	n/a
The preacher showed evidence of biblical study.						
Biblical material was applied to contemporary life.						
The sermon was well-organized and flowed well.						
The sermon had one central theme/idea.						
The sermon had a strong introduction.						
The sermon had a strong conclusion.						
The sermon had appropriate transitions.						
The preacher chose appropriate illustrations.						
The sermon was relevant for me.						
The preacher was not overly nervous.						
The preacher showed creative use of imagination.						
The preacher spoke with appropriate volume.						
The preacher varied his/her pitch and tone.						
The preacher's delivery rate was appropriate.						
The preacher made good eye contact.						
The preacher used appropriate gestures.						
The preacher used notes/manuscript appropriately.						
The preacher was passionate and engaged.						
The preacher was dressed appropriately.						

What images/phrases stood out to you in
the message?

Name one specific thing the preacher did
well in his/her message.

Name one specific growth point for the
preacher.

What new personal insights/learnings/
challenges did you gain from this
message?

THE IMPORTANCE OF PREACHING COLLEAGUES

Every minister needs a support network, and a peer group dedicated to preaching can be an invaluable resource. A preaching peer group works best when it is lectionary based, because everyone is working on the same passages, but they can be very valuable even if the preachers are working on different texts. Some peer groups are multidenominational, and local pastors will gather early each week to share resources and process where they might be going with next Sunday's message. Perhaps you are part of such a group, and you can invite your intern to join you as often as it is practical.

Other groups are more homogenous, and they may gather in an online forum. Several popular preaching websites have weekly lectionary-based text discussions that can be helpful. Assist your intern in identifying and engaging with these resources.

Other peer groups meet two to three times a year to plan preaching and worship well in advance. One such group of Baptist pastors has gathered semiannually for many years now. They meet for several days of "preacher camp," where they plan, resource, and preach (with peer critique) for each other. At the end of the work sessions, their families often join them for a few days of rest and play. Each person in this group will testify to the ways they have benefited personally and professionally from this long-term relationship. Encourage your interns to seek out and offer peer support throughout their preaching careers.

READ WIDELY, PREACH CONTEXTUALLY

One of the best ways we can help novice preachers is to encourage them to read widely: newspapers (in print or online), journals, novels, poetry, nonfiction, commentaries, and blogs. Young preachers tend to draw heavily on their own experiences for illustrations, and reading widely will help them broaden and deepen their pool of illustrative material.

The next step then is to help our students translate this depth and breadth of knowledge into their specific preaching contexts. Every time they preach ask them, "Where is the intersection between your scriptural text, what is happening in the larger world, and what this congregation needs to hear on this particular Sunday?" This intersection is where the best sermons happen.

BALANCING PROPHETIC AND PASTORAL PREACHING

Do you lean toward prophetic or pastoral preaching? Which does your student prefer? Regardless of our personal preference, the well-rounded preacher must discern which type of sermon is appropriate on a given Sunday. It is essential, but extremely difficult, to preach prophetically in our deeply polarized society. Prophetic sermons on difficult social issues are essential, but they should be an invitation to deeper dialogue and discussion, not an opportunity for the preacher to deliver a tongue-lashing or shame the congregation. See the list of resources below for books that provide excellent guidance in this area.

BATHE IT ALL IN PRAYER

We can teach our students a lot about the art and craft of preaching, but it will all be for naught if we fail to bathe the entire enterprise in prayer. Encourage your students to pray before they begin sermon prep and frequently through the process. Pray for your students as they learn, and pray with them regularly—but especially right before worship. Knowing that someone is covering you in prayer can calm nerves and boost confidence. Most important, prayer reminds us that we do not engage in this important ministry on our own.

QUESTIONS FOR REFLECTION

1. Mentors, as a young preacher, who or what helped you grow as you developed your own voice for preaching?
2. Of the principles discussed above, which are you using already to mentor your students? Which others might you need to add to your supervisory conversations?
3. Does your congregation need training on how to mentor a novice preacher? How can you help them learn to help your student?

SUGGESTED READINGS

Holbert, John, and Alyce McKenzie. *What Not to Say: Avoiding the Common Mistakes That Can Sink Your Sermon.* Louisville, KY: Westminster John Knox Press, 2011.

McMickle, Marvin. *Where Have all the Prophets Gone? Reclaiming Prophetic Preaching in America.* Cleveland, OH: Pilgrim, 2006.

Schade, Leah D. *Preaching in the Purple Zone: Ministry in the Red-Blue Divide.* Lanham, MD: Rowman & Littlefield, 2019.

Tisdale, Leonora Tubbs. *Prophetic Preaching: A Pastoral Approach.* Louisville, KY: Westminster John Knox Press, 2011.

Tisdale, Leonora Tubbs, and Thomas H. Troeger. *A Sermon Workbook: Exercises in the Art and Craft of Preaching.* Nashville: Abingdon, 2013.

Chapter Twenty-Two

Mentoring the Administrator

Thomas L. Fuller

When you discerned a call to ministry leadership and took those initial steps to pursue formal training for ministry, you probably had mental images or visions of yourself functioning in a ministerial capacity. You may have envisioned preaching the word of God to an assembled congregation, comforting a grieving family, discipling a new believer, or providing leadership to missional endeavors. If you are like me, however, those early visions of ministry probably did not include scenes of meetings with the finance committee, performing staff evaluations, or developing policies for the use of church facilities. Yet, we both discovered all too quickly that ministry, in its many forms, requires or entails some amount of administrative support, coordination, and oversight. In fact, in their weekly work, ministry leaders report spending the third greatest amount of time on administrative matters— exceeded only by time spent preparing for preaching and worship and providing pastoral care. [1]

Your student needs your help to prepare for this ministry of administration. They need not only to be informed about the time and attention it will require (which probably is more than they anticipate), but prepared and equipped for faithful and competent service. You can help to facilitate that preparation by assisting your student to gain

- a basic understanding of administrative processes,
- a healthy perspective toward the work of administration, and
- a good feel for the minister's role in administrative affairs.

There is no better way for that learning and growth to take place than for the student to observe and engage in the practice of ministry under your competent and caring supervision.

GAINING A BASIC UNDERSTANDING OF
ADMINISTRATIVE PROCESSES

So, how can you help your students to become competent administrators? As with several other areas of ministry leadership, competency in administration is both art and science; it is a combination of knowledge, understanding, and skill, as well as wisdom, maturity, and grace. Your students need to learn not only how to read and understand a financial report or to prepare an agenda and lead a meeting, but how to function administratively with pastoral sensitivity and theological vision. You play a vital role in that learning process as you provide instruction and new opportunities, as you facilitate theological reflection and share your insights, and as you model ministry for them.

The goal, of course, is for the minister in training to gain a basic understanding of administrative processes through hands-on experience. However, it can be a real challenge for students to get that kind of experience with administration in their field education placements. Most ministry internship sites do not afford students the opportunities for administrative practice that are ultimately necessary to gain real competency. In many instances, this is understandable. In light of this, it is important that you find and create ways for your students to gain an understanding of—and where possible, some skills for—ministry administration.

One of the simplest ways to facilitate this learning is to allow your students to sit in on meetings in which administrative matters are being discussed or handled. Subject to what the context and circumstances allow, a student could benefit from observing a meeting(s) of the

- church or ministry staff
- governing board or body (and/or a congregational business meeting, if applicable)
- finance committee (especially when developing an annual budget)
- personnel committee
- property committee

Students also have shared with me the value they sometimes find in meeting with or interviewing various people who are involved with administrative processes, such as the treasurer or financial secretary, the building coordinator, or a ministry director. Besides learning about the nature of their work, it can be a good opportunity to ask questions such as, "What do you wish members of the pastoral staff knew about what you do?" or "How can the pastoral staff and other ministry leaders best support you in the work you do?" Students may derive similar benefits from speaking with members of the pastoral staff to ask about the nature and scope of administration involved in their work.

What the students learn by observation and interviews can provide the raw material for additional learning in your supervisory meetings with them. You can assess what has been learned and where gaps remain, clarify or correct misunderstandings, share the wisdom of experience, and facilitate theological reflection. With these things in mind, I suggest that you have your students develop at least two questions to bring to the supervisory meeting that follows any such experience.

These practices may enhance students' understanding of administration, but they will not help them develop skills. That requires engagement. At some point during students' supervised ministry experience, you should consider giving them leadership responsibility for a ministry project or event (or at least for some component thereof). It should require interfacing with the broadest range of administrative functions—from planning and organizing to recruiting and staffing, from budgeting and promoting to executing and evaluating—and it should be something that stretches the students' administrative capacities beyond their existing limits. To the extent possible, your involvement should be limited to being a resource and guide, allowing the students to have ownership of the project, to learn from the experience, and to gain confidence in their administrative abilities.

DEVELOPING A HEALTHY PERSPECTIVE TOWARD ADMINISTRATION

How do your students regard the work of administration as a part of ministry leadership? This may take some time to discern. They may be coming to ministry as a second career after several years of experience in the corporate sector with a lot of confidence in their administrative abilities but little appreciation for the nuances of administration in the pastoral office. Or they may be young and passionate for the advancement of the gospel, with little patience for the perceived (and sometimes real) bureaucracies of planning, budgeting, managing, reporting, and evaluating but find themselves serving in a context with those firmly established practices. You must take them where they are and walk with them patiently to develop a healthy—or healthier—perspective toward the administrative dimensions of ministry leadership. Several components lead to a healthy perspective toward ministry administration, but I will mention only three that deserve consideration.

Administration is ministry. Faith communities across the ages have encountered the reality that shared life and mission require attention to matters of organization, resources, planning, and functioning. This is reflected at several points throughout the scriptures, from the ways that God ordered the liturgical and cultic life of the tabernacle (Exodus 25–31) to the manner in which the early church in Jerusalem responded to a problem of distributing food and care to the widows among them (Acts 6:1–7). As with all matters of ministry, God has gifted the body for the work of administration (1 Corinthians 12:27–28). You should encourage your students to regard administration as a legitimate part of faithful ministry leadership, especially if they are inclined to treat it as a bothersome distraction. Be mindful of the example you set in this regard, as students commonly will take their cues from you.

Administration is a means to an end. Although some students and ministers may fail to appreciate that administration is ministry, others may give it inordinate priority and attention to the neglect of more necessary ministry responsibilities. Eugene Peterson points to this as one of the distinguishing marks of "religious shopkeeping."[2] Similarly, Colin Marshall and Tony Payne warn against giving too much attention to the "trellis" of administration, to the neglect of tending the "vine" of proclaiming the gospel and making disciples.[3] Administration is a valid, valuable, and necessary ministry, but it is not an end in itself. It makes possible and supports the central work of glorifying God, proclaiming the gospel, and building up the body of Christ. This is one of many things in ministry leadership that you can help your students to hold in proper tension.

Administration is more about running a household than running a business. The fact is that the administration of Christian ministry involves plenty of organizational and business-related matters. Those preparing for ministry leadership do well to acquire an appropriate degree of working knowledge about such matters. After all, it is important that we do not spend beyond the resources we have, that we establish and follow sound policies and procedures for personnel management, and that we practice good stewardship by maintaining the physical resources that God has entrusted to us. In Christian ministry, however, such things as "the bottom line," key performance indicators (KPIs), and measures/metrics of success should not be solely defined in terms of efficiency and productivity. In the scriptures, the church is described in familial terms (John 1:12; Ephesians 1:5; 1 John 3:1–2) and as a household (Galatians 6:10; Ephesians 2:19; 1 Timothy 3:15). Good administrative practices should contribute to the soundness of the household and the well-being of the family that resides in it. You can help your students understand that the house and its affairs exist for the people who do life together in it, not the other way around. And both exist to serve the purposes of God.

NEGOTIATING THE MINISTER'S ROLE IN ADMINISTRATION

Students' perspective toward administration, among other things, will influence how they understand the minister's role in administration. This is one piece of the puzzle we refer to as pastoral identity: one's understanding of what it means to be and to function as a pastor. At one end of the spectrum is the CEO or manager model of ministry, with the minister hyper-involved in administrative affairs, likely to the neglect of other pastoral duties. At the other end of the spectrum is the minister who is totally disconnected from any and all matters of administration. Although some may find that appealing, it commonly contributes to problems and dysfunction in planning, communication, supervision, and other facets of the community's life and work. So, what is the Goldilocks level of engagement in administration for a minister? And how do you help your students find it?

No one right level of engagement in administration applies to every minister in every ministry context, which is why this is a matter to be negotiated. Your students' personality type, gifts, and background bear consideration. One may be naturally inclined to the work of administration, or bring some valuable skills and experience to contribute. Then again, a student may be organizationally challenged and ill-equipped to function administratively.

The ministry context is another variable in the equation. How complex or well-developed are the administrative structure and practices of the church or ministry organization? What expectations administratively does the church or ministry organization have of ministerial staff members? Situational or seasonal factors must be considered. The church initiates a capital campaign for an addition to the facilities. Disciplinary action is required in response to misconduct by a staff member. These exigencies require a minister's involvement in a way that supersedes other considerations.

Most of the work of negotiating their role in administration will take place after your students have graduated and entered into full-time service in ministry. But in this season of supervised ministry, you can help students prepare for it. First, you can make them aware that their administrative role or level of engagement *is* something to be negotiated. Otherwise, they may experience a great deal of discouragement or guilt when their capacities do not match perfectly with every demand of the first position they hold.

Second, you can help your students gain an understanding of the scope of administrative responsibilities that you have in your role. More important, share and discuss with them how you negotiated your level of engagement with those responsibilities. Your story may not be a textbook example of how to do it, but students will benefit from hearing about your successes as well as your failures.

And, third, seize opportunities to engage your students in reflection on ministry models and pastoral identity. In years to come, when the students must answer the question, "What is my role as a ministry leader in this administrative matter?," they can respond best if equipped with a healthy, biblical understanding of the life and work of pastoral ministry and with insight into how God has gifted them to serve most effectively.

QUESTIONS FOR REFLECTION

1. In light of the fact that administrative roles and responsibilities can vary from one ministry context to another, which administrative principles, processes, and practices do you deem to be most common to ministry leadership across contexts?
2. Has your perspective toward ministry administration changed over time? If so, how?
3. Which resources or practices have you found most helpful in negotiating your role as an administrator?

SUGGESTED READINGS

Dockery, David S., ed. *Christian Leadership Essentials: A Handbook for Managing Christian Organizations.* Nashville: B&H Academic, 2011.

Gangel, Kenneth O. *Feeding and Leading: A Practical Handbook on Administration in Churches and Christian Organizations.* Grand Rapids, MI: Baker, 1989.

Lawson, Kevin E., and Mick Boersma. *Supervising and Supporting Ministry Staff: A Guide to Thriving Together.* Lanham, MD: Rowman & Littlefield, 2017.

Veith, Gene Edward, Jr. *God at Work: Your Christian Vocation in All of Life.* Wheaton, IL: Crossway, 2002.

Weeks, Louis B. *All for God's Glory: Redeeming Church Scutwork.* Herndon, VA: Alban, 2008.

Chapter Twenty-Three

Mentoring the Pastoral Caregiver

Susan MacAlpine-Gillis

How long has it been since you began your journey in pastoral ministry? Do you remember when pastoral care was new and every day brought something you had never experienced before? Do you remember that combination of terror and excitement? It has been more than thirty-five years, and I still remember how I felt setting out on this new adventure working with a supervisor-mentor. I was young, inexperienced, and terrified that someone would die. How would I know what to do? My "Introduction to Pastoral Care" course seemed woefully inadequate. I remember praying, "Please, God, just don't let anybody die!"

I'm sure you can guess how that worked out—13 funerals in 16 weeks and 5 funerals in 7 days while my supervisor was away on vacation. In one of my first supervision sessions, I remember confessing my fear of funerals to my supervisor-mentor. His response is one I have worked hard to model when students have shared their fears with me: to listen without judgment. Then he helped me explore my concerns, offered me tools, and invited me to accompany him as he met with families in grief situations. I observed the way he navigated the unpredictable spaces of grief to offer pastoral care and to gather important information to plan the funeral. He shared a method for preparing a funeral sermon, and with the permission of the family, invited me to participate in the funeral.

The most important element was the opportunity to reflect on the experience after the fact. What had I learned? How did I see God at work? How was I being formed for ministry through this event? How was my theology of death and resurrection being expressed? As I became more comfortable, he invited me to take the lead, and I gained knowledge and confidence. I still hoped nobody would die when he went on vacation, but when the phone call came from the funeral home, I felt somewhat prepared.

159

Pastoral care is an art. Your students will need tools, guidance, opportunities to hone their skills, and, most important, a safe place to reflect on and learn from those experiences. This is especially true of those experiences where things did not go as your student had hoped.

As one of my former students wrote:

> A true growing edge was to learn that despite best intentions, mistakes happened with all of us, and even the possibility of "failure" was not the end. By learning to give situations my best and accepting that even my best might not achieve the results I hoped for, I came to accept mistakes as opportunities to listen, learn and grow. The freedom to admit mistakes and then hear and contemplate collegial perspectives in a safe and respectful way was invaluable.

As a supervisor-mentor, one of your most important roles is to help your student identify their growing edges—what do they need to learn? Every student is different, but I have never met a student who did not have some level of fear related to pastoral care—fear of doing something wrong, fear of saying something wrong, fear of not having something to say.

> F-E-A-R: has two meanings: Forget Everything And Run or Face Everything And Rise. The choice is yours.
>
> —Zig Ziglar

Your role is to support the second option and help your students rise to any occasion. Remember the encouraging words in Philippians 4:13, "I can do all things through Christ who strengthens me." Students need to be reassured that it is God who works through them and to make space for the Holy.

Here are three areas of growth common for most students:

1. to understand that pastoral care is not about fixing things—it is about being present and bearing witness to faith in God's Grace and Hope
2. to understand the role of prayer in a pastoral situation and become comfortable praying with people
3. how to move a visit from purely social to more deeply pastoral and theological

PASTORAL CARE IS NOT ABOUT FIXING THINGS

A former intern wrote:

> One "learning edge" I had around pastoral care was overcoming my desire to try to "fix" a problem or do something concrete in response to someone's pain or crisis, etc. as though my role was to make things better or ok. I remember an exercise in a grief workshop in seminary where we had to listen to someone

describe at length a conflict or experience of grief without commenting, inter-
rupting or speaking at all—learning to actively listen and realizing that listening and witnessing in and of themselves are healing and spiritual practices,
something meaningful to offer people in distress.

Our human instinct is to do *something* to fix the problem, and yet in many
situations that simply is not possible. You can help your students sit in those
places of discomfort and simply be. You can model active listening and
compassionate care. You can teach the benefit of silence and the healing
power of appropriate touch, offered with permission: holding a hand, a pat on
a shoulder, even a hug. Pastoral care theory can be taught, but the opportunity to observe pastoral care in action and reflect on the experience is incredibly valuable for students.

It's hard for anxious students to let the visit be about the other person.
Instead of entering deeply into what the person is saying and feeling, they are
scrambling to think how they will respond. As a supervisor-mentor, you can
reflect with your students on where they were during the visit, and more
important, what was going on for the other person. How did the student, as
the pastoral caregiver, enter the experience of the other?

It is also important to discern the presence and movement of the Spirit for
both the person being visited and the student. Where were the Holy moments?

The ministry of presence is not about doing, fixing, solving, or making
better. It is about being. It is about letting the other know that they are not
alone. God's loving action in the world is made known through our loving
action. We embody the presence of the Spirit of God. We are called to be a
non-anxious presence, an oasis of calm during the storm, a refuge, a rock, a
place of shelter and support.

Think about how you prepare yourself spiritually. Do you have a prayer
practice or a ritual that grounds you and reminds you that is it God who
works through you? Share that with your students. Often, I ground myself
through singing. If I am alone in the car, voicing my prayer in song as I drive
is helpful.

The ideas and practices you share with your students will be formative for
them as they develop confidence and proficiency in this important aspect of
ministry.

THE PLACE OF PRAYER

The number one learning goal for most of my students is becoming comfortable with extemporaneous prayer. I can still remember the way anxiety
would manifest itself in my body when I thought I should offer prayer with
someone, a sinking feeling in the pit of my stomach, clammy hands, rapid

breath. To be honest, even after I was ordained I would do just about anything to avoid praying with someone. I understand the apprehension of students. In my training, none of my supervisor-mentors pushed me to pray; yet
prayer is one of those things that you will never become comfortable doing
unless you do it. I often have wondered if my supervisor-mentors were also
uncomfortable with prayer. The move from rehearsing the words of prayer in
your mind to allowing the words of prayer to flow from an engaged heart is
critical for students. As supervisor-mentors it is difficult to teach people to
pray, but you can make space for prayer as part of supervision sessions,
alternating who begins and who ends your time with prayer.

The more times students pray extemporaneously in a safe space, the more
proficient they become. As one experienced supervisor-mentor wrote, "I try
to teach people to pray, rather than to say a bunch of stuff that sounds like a
prayer and to say 'amen' when they're done rather than 'uhm' as they scram-
ble for what else to say."

As a supervisor-mentor it is important to explore with students ways to
invite prayer into pastoral visits that make it natural and less intimidating but
also give people the language to decline respectfully: "Would you like me to
pray with you now, or would you rather not at this time?" We should never
assume that people want us to pray with them, nor should we impose our
desire to pray over the wishes of the one being visited. We can always make
the offer. Although prayer often is seen by students as a way to bring a visit
to an end, the very act of prayer can break down barriers and unleash new
expressions of emotion that need to be processed before the visit is concluded. Offering to pray before the time that you expect the visit to end can
be helpful and allow time for the unexpected.

An alternative to prayer in those public spaces where privacy and noise
can make prayer awkward is to offer a blessing—to lay your hand on someone, with their permission, look them in the eye and bless them naming their
situation and desires.

WHAT MAKES A VISIT PASTORAL?

A former student wrote,

> I came to acknowledge that when I make a pastoral visit as a minister I am
> representing the congregation and God in some small way. I am a physical
> reminder that the faith community and God care about this person and situa-
> tion—my office represented something to people that was different than a visit
> from a church friend. And that's where developing a habit of offering prayer at
> pastoral visits is so important. In prayer you are intentionally invoking and
> drawing attention to God's presence.

Talk with your student about the role they have when they visit on behalf of the congregation. Your modeling and coaching will help your student engage in pastoral conversations that talk about God, reflect theologically, and invite the other person to reflect on the deeper questions that may be lingering in his mind and heart. We come as those who are trained to bridge the gap between the experiences of our lives and the faith and traditions that ground our way of being in the world.

Students need to be comfortable wading deeply into the big topics of life. Help them identify areas where they are not comfortable and take time to talk about them.

An experienced supervisor-mentor wrote,

> I took a student to the hospital with me to see a woman who was in her final days. There was no one else there and the woman wasn't responsive, and I just talked. The student was shocked that I talked to her about death. Students tend to avoid the real pastoral concern and wait for the other person to raise it. I raise it and if there is a resistance to talking about it, I will back off a bit. Often people don't know how to begin the conversation.

Learning how to weave theological reflection into the fabric of pastoral visits, to help those they are visiting make connections between what is happening in their life and their faith, is a gift that you can give.

In *A Primer in Pastoral Care*, Jeanne Stevenson-Moessner writes about the Grammar of Care. You might want to reflect on your POSTURE as you mentor your students toward proficiency in pastoral care.[1]

Posture

P Pray with your students and for each other. Provide opportunities for practice. None of us become proficient in pastoral care without the opportunity to provide care in a variety of places. Push your students to identify their growing edges.

O Be open with your students about your growing edges. Take some time to remember what it was like when you were being formed in ministry. Observe your students as they offer pastoral care and let them observe you.

S Make sure you are spiritually grounded when you meet for supervision and share spiritual practices that are part of your tool kit for pastoral care. Judiciously share stories from your pastoral ministry and what you learned from that experience.

T Build trust with your students and teach your students to trust themselves. Incorporate theological reflection into your supervision time so that together you make connections between faith and experience.

U Be understanding as you and your students embark on this new adventure. "Help me understand" can invite deeper conversation.

R Build the foundation of a respectful relationship with your students. Be free in sharing resources and consider role playing as a teaching tool.

E Be an engaged supervisor who encourages your students to experiment and to say "Yes" to new experiences.

As a supervisor-mentor you have a wonderful opportunity to work with students as they discover their pastoral identity and hone their pastoral skills. Through the sharing of your wisdom and experience, new students can gain confidence and experience. As you take on this important ministry, remember your own experience of learning a new task.

I remember when my grandmother taught me to make bread. She gave me the list of ingredients and told me the order in which to put them together. Then she told me to "knead it till it feels right." The first time you make bread, you have no idea what it is supposed to feel like. With opportunities to practice with good supervision from an experienced bread maker, and sometimes failing, you discover just exactly what that means. Pastoral care is similar—you need to do it until it feels right: you know the ingredients, you no longer need to look at the recipe, and it becomes second nature.

QUESTIONS FOR REFLECTION

1. What were your biggest fears around pastoral care? Did you have a supervisor who helped you address those fears? If so, how? How might you use your personal experience to mentor students?
2. What spiritual practices do you use to ground yourself in God as you offer pastoral care?
3. Could any aspects of your POSTURE for mentoring use attention?

SUGGESTED READINGS

Ashley, Willard Walden Christopher, Sr. "Engaging in Pastoral Care." In *Engage: A Theological Field Education Toolkit*, edited by Matthew Floding. Lanham, MD: Rowman & Littlefield, 2017.

Paton, John. *Pastoral Care an Essential Guide*. Nashville: Abingdon, 2005.

Stevenson-Moessner, Jeanne. *A Primer in Pastoral Care*. Minneapolis, MN: Augsburg Fortress, 2005.

Chapter Twenty-Four

Mentoring for Faith Formation

Sung Hee Chang

Welcome to "the [strange] *new* world" (à la Karl Barth) within the field of faith formation in which you are called by God to be a supervisor-mentor. The world of the mentor-mentee relationship is neither yours nor the mentees'; it is, like the world within the Bible, "a new world, the world of God." Just as "[i]t is not the right human thoughts about God which form the content of the Bible, but the right divine thoughts about men [and women],"[1] so the right question for you to ask is not how you and your mentees, respectively and collectively, would understand faith formation but how God would form your faith as well as your mentees' in this *new* relationship.

If you think you are able and even qualified to teach others to do ministry because you have done ministry well at your ministerial setting, you are quite mistaken. First of all, you must be aware and admit that ministering and mentoring are entirely different things. A "good" minister does not necessarily turn out to be a "good" mentor. You may be an expert in ministering. And yet you could be a novice in mentoring. Further, you need to remind yourself whenever you mentor your mentees that, like many field educators, you just "stumbled into" or "fell into" the mentoring job without knowing what you are really getting into and without fully figuring out "the move from doing to teaching about doing." This move from ministering to mentoring requires of you humility and wisdom.[2]

The good news is that to mentor is God's call, just as to minister is. What is unique about this seemingly new call is that while God is calling someone else to minister by calling you to mentor the person, God is still calling you to continue to minister. For, just as an artist does in teaching his or her art, you supervise and mentor "by the very act of ministering." You never stop being a minister whose proper posture is what Charlene Jin Lee calls "a *posture* of being and becoming," as one of *limmudim*, "those who are taught [by God]" (Isaiah 50:4, NRSV). What you engage, knowingly or unknowingly, in the mentor-mentee relationship, therefore, is faith formation. The baseline to be established is this: "Formation is a necessary activity for all who are responding to God's call," both for you and for your mentee.[3]

WHAT IS MENTORING FOR FAITH FORMATION REALLY ABOUT?

Elsewhere I presented four points concerning your meaningful engagement in faith formation: its God-centeredness, context-specificity, whole community scope, and engaged process.[4] I believe these points are important for your reflection on *mentoring for faith formation as a significant component of your responding to God's call*. In this chapter, I would like to offer the following four points that address respectively the *why, who, for what*, and *how* of mentoring in the engaged process of God's contextual and communal formation of our faith.

First, *mentoring is a calling and everyone's business*. Do not think you alone are special and privileged. Everyone means not only all but also *any*. When people are asked about "all those who have helped them become who they are" (à la Fred Rogers of the TV show *Mister Rogers' Neighborhood*), many of them, after pausing for a minute of silence in remembrance and gratitude, would name some "unlikely mentors" who helped their faith survive the unhospitable world and even the unwelcoming church.[5] It is most unlikely that many of these mentors named would identify themselves as mentors. They did not choose to be mentors. Rather, they were chosen, not only by God but also by their mentees. Therefore, when you are called to serve as a mentor, remember that you do not choose your mentee. And recall what your own mentors did for you—they lovingly ministered to you just as Jesus ministered to his disciples, his mentees. In a nutshell, according to Leona M. English, who studied the historical and spiritual basis of the mentor-mentee relationship, "providing mentorship [is] a Christian responsibility."[6] Christian discipleship necessarily involves mentoring. As you serve as a mentor, you are doing just what you are supposed to do. Nothing more, nothing less.

Second, *mentors are not above mentees, and the mentor-mentee relationship should be mutual*. The traditional idea of mentoring was hierarchical, if not authoritarian. The mentor was believed to represent the authoritative tradition of wisdom, and the mentee was expected to obey and follow the wise mentor. Mentoring practices in the biblical wisdom tradition, in general, follow this line of thinking.[7] And yet, that is not necessarily the only biblical understanding of the mentor-mentee relationship.

For example, John 15:12–15 reveals "the kind of relationship for which every mentee hopes and toward which every mentor should aim: Jesus and those who follow him are *friends*."[8] The "[M]aster's business" (John 15:15) was and still is building a special relationship, that is, friendship with his mentees. Like friendship, the mentor-mentee relationship can be formed in a way that both the mentor and the mentee can learn and grow together. This kind of mentoring is called "co-mentoring." It replaces the traditional "image of a master forming an apprentice in something of his own image" with the feminist image of a midwife "[coaching] the mentee in birthing what she (or he) has to offer to the world."[9] Seen from this perspective of mutuality, mentors are "not experts, but good companions on the road who have lived with the questions that discipleship inevitably raises and who have found treasure hidden and shared in some unlikely fields."[10] In essence, mentors and mentees are fellow travelers/pilgrims whose common journey has to do with "the transformation of personal character in the search for sanctity [or perfection]"[11] or "the formation of a [humane] disposition, style, or stance in life."[12]

Third, *what mentors and mentees must recover during their common journey of mentorship is the joy of ministry.* Do not pretend that the holy transformation or humane formation of personal character is your business. It is God's. What you need to do instead, advises Thomas Currie, is to keep in mind, and remind your mentee, of the fact that "there seems to be a lack of wonder or sense of mystery or wellspring of joy that accompanies and sustains Christian ministry today."[13] Barth once said, "The theologian who has no joy in his [or her] work is not a theologian at all."[14] This statement rings true to a minister and further to a Christian. Joy is the identity marker for the Christian and joyful obedience for Christian ministry. Joy should be your and your mentee's bread for the common journey for faith formation. Whenever you feel burdened with your duty of mentoring, therefore, seek the joy of ministry and its source, God's love, with your mentee.

Fourth, *both mentors and mentees should understand one another's ways of learning.* This is important, because we often forget that people learn differently. To learn together, you have to learn about your mentee's ways of learning just as your mentee has to learn about your ways of learning. Contemporary learning research has drawn our attention to the fact that "students' achievement increases when teaching methods match their learning styles—biological and developmental characteristics that affect how they learn." Notably, "[m]ost children can master the same content; *how* they master it is determined by their individual styles."[15] The same conclusion can be made regarding adult learners with one major caveat: that the learner's learning style is not only biological and developmental but also contextual and communal. That is to say, the learner learns not only as an individual but also as one who belongs to a learning community. And, like individuals, different communities have employed different ways of learning. Therefore, it is important for all "co-learners," that is, both for your mentees and for you as mentor (and the mentoring group) to note that a mismatch between the learner's learning style and that of a new learning community in which the learner gets placed could impede the learning of the learner as well as that of your learning community.

SOME PRACTICAL ADVICE REGARDING MENTORING FOR FAITH FORMATION

As I wish you all the best in your "ever ancient, ever new" (à la Augustine of Hippo) journey of mentoring for faith formation, I offer my two cents' worth of counsel:

- *Pray with and for your mentee and praise God together whenever you spend time with your mentee.* The mentoring you should be concerned with is not an academic or ministerial business, let alone a corporate business; it is a *spiritual* business. A most-sought academic mentor of spirituality, whose driving force in life was being successful and who was restless constantly, once sought help from a monk mentor at a Trappist monastery as he lived there as a "temporary Trappist." The latter taught the former that prayer is a way of life. At the end the former came to realize that "a monastery is not built to solve problems but to praise the Lord in the midst of them."[16] The same is true for mentoring. Engage in any spiritual disciplines that would enable you and your mentee to focus the mind on God's faith formation. Remember that God has called you and your mentee to be faithful, not to be successful (à la Mother Teresa).
- *Help your mentee to discern God's call.* Mentoring primarily concerns discerning God's call at this particular moment of the mentee's life. And yet God never stops calling God's people. Accordingly, you should help your mentee to have "a lifelong perspective" on the process of discerning God's calling in time and space.[17] By doing this, just as the baptized members are revisiting their own baptism during the liturgy for the Reaffirmation of Baptism, you are also examining the faithfulness of your vocation.
- *Pause and ponder to pay attention to the presence of God and behold what God is doing in the world and in the church, particularly in the mentor-mentee relationship, by "practicing spiritual companioning."* What is suggested here goes beyond the traditional "practice of the presence of God" (à la Brother Lawrence) and the biblical practice of beholding. It is to "[view] the course of life as a spiritual journey" and gather the stories of your mentee, reflect on them in light of life course theory, and

help your mentee to connect them to biblical stories.[18] For this spiritual practice of accompaniment, you need to, first, learn about the method of storytelling and story weaving and, second, recognize that your mentee has the necessary resources for theological reasoning already formed before you two met.

- *Build an abiding relationship with your mentee and create a safe space where both you and your mentee can feel confident of not being judged.* The word *mentor* came from the Greek word *meno*, which means to abide or remain. To the mentees who do not know much about what is coming, it is the good news that you intend to stay with them on the common journey for God's faith formation. To begin the journey together, building a reliable relationship and creating a safe space is a must and that is your job as the mentor, not your mentees'. Once you accomplish this task, you and your mentees will engage "a fierce, focused, continuing conversation in which a mentor, attempting to be helpful to a protégé [mentee], is helped."[19]

- *Ask some questions that would lead your mentees to unlearn what they have learned.* It is a truism among ministers and educators that it is more difficult to teach the faith to those who have already learned than to those who have not learned. Learning without unlearning and relearning is a petrified learning that is unable to advance. And when you disrupt the equilibrium of your mentees with questions of unlearning, you should remember that what goes around comes around. You have to unlearn yourself, too.[20]

- *Get engaged in intercultural learning and intergenerational learning.* Unlearning also happens when you move out of your safe zone of learning. Both intercultural learning and intergenerational learning could help you to understand that your safe zone and that of your mentee are not big enough—not big enough to contain God's love and cover God's mission. Know that beyond your safe zone lies not only your fear zone but also what Eric Law calls *the grace margin* that "provides time and space for [you] to maintain an openness to explore—to listen and discover and reflect." Law imagines that in this *place* of unlearning and relearning among the dancers, that is, mentors and mentees, Christ choreographs in a way that He "reorders [their] relationships with one another and with God."[21]

QUESTIONS FOR REFLECTION

1. What does a minister have to keep in mind when called to mentor others in faith formation process?

2. How can the mentor and the mentees recover together the joy of educational ministry?
3. In the co-mentoring relationship, what is required of both mentors and mentees?
4. What kinds of ways of learning need to be studied urgently at your ministerial context?

SUGGESTED READINGS

Currie, Thomas W., III. *The Joy of Ministry*. Louisville, KY: Westminster John Knox, 2008.
Daloz, Laurent A. *Mentor: Guiding the Journey of Adult Learners*. San Francisco: Jossey-Bass, 1999.
English, Leona M. *Mentoring in Religious Education*. Birmingham, AL: Religious Education Press, 1998.
Kocher, Craig T., Jason Byassee, and James C. Howell, eds. *Mentoring for Ministry: The Grace of Growing Pastors*. Eugene, OR: Cascade, 2017.
Thompson, Dean K., and D. Cameron Murchison, eds. *Mentoring: Biblical, Theological, and Practical Perspectives*. Grand Rapids, MI: Eerdmans, 2018.

Chapter Twenty-Five

Mentoring for Public Leadership and Social Change

Melissa Browning

It was the end of the spring semester when a first-year seminary student stopped by my office. She leaned into the doorway nervously, unsure as to whether it was safe to sit down. She had a question, she said, but it was unclear to me in this awkward moment whether she would find the courage to ask it.

Then she began to gush, "I was told I should talk to you, that I have to talk to you, that you're the only one who teaches this class, but I really don't want to take your class. Not yet, at least. I mean, I know you make all your students protest and I'm not ready for that. Not yet. Do I have to protest to take your course? I just want to do an internship at my church!"

My response probably did not calm her nerves, "You're thinking of my other courses," I replied. "Protesting is not a requirement for contextual education, though maybe it should be!"

To be fair, she wasn't wrong. As a contextual education professor with a community development and community organizing background, I always look for ways to help my students take to the streets and create social change. That semester I was teaching an elective course on mass incarceration and restorative justice where students were required to stand vigil in protest each time the state of Georgia executed another one of God's children. Our seminary was still reeling from Kelly Gissendaner's death, and many of our students had been active in the campaign to save her from execution. As one of the organizers on that campaign, I knew my teaching had to honor her life and legacy, and my students agreed that because of Kelly, this class had to be more than content taught in a classroom. So, we agreed to stand vigil together, to march together, to protest together—all for course credit. But what seemed like a way to honor Kelly at the beginning of the semester soon became too much. In three short months, five people were killed by the state of Georgia. Two of these people were closely tied to my students. One went to high school with a student in my class, the other was being defended by a law professor at our university. The requirement to stand vigil became optional as the near-weekly executions began to weigh on our emotional health.

Mentoring students for public leadership and social change can be exhausting and difficult work. But it is good work, if you can find it. Some students, such as my nervous visitor, are not yet ready to engage. Others make bold and ambitious plans but burn out before the internship is over. Most students are somewhere in between, with a deeply rooted desire to create change intertwined with the helpless feeling that change will never come.

When we commit to a relationship in which we are mentoring or being mentored, no scientific formula will make our work magically produce results. No mentoring happens without risk, no success without the very real possibility of failure. Although I cannot give you a formula for success, I can point to a few postures that are well suited to mentoring students who want to be part of a transforming community.

WHERE TO BEGIN? WITH THE GIFTS OF THE COMMUNITY

First things first: we must *start with gifts*. My friend John McKnight, one of the founders of Asset-based Community Development, often says, "You can't do anything with a need, so why start there?" Organizers and other changemakers can become cynical really fast. We're doing the never-ending work of (attempting to) deconstruct injustice, and we know where all of the bodies are buried. In the midst of seeing all that is wrong, we sometimes forget that every person, every community, and every neighborhood is brimming to the rim with gifts and capacities to create its own change. When we begin with an asset-based approach, both in naming the gifts of the students we mentor and pointing out the gifts of the neighborhoods where they will work, we practice a theology of abundance rather than scarcity. In naming gifts, we abandon the narrative of hopelessness and find that God has given us ample tools for the journey. Starting with gifts does not mean we ignore what is wrong, but it does mean that we resist the temptation to label people or drown in our own deficit thinking.

In the same way, the best mentors allow community folks, brimming with all of their giftedness, to be the student's teacher. Great mentors *let the community be the teacher*. When you commit to mentoring for social change, part of your job is to introduce and step aside. If you're working with a community experiencing homelessness, celebrate the gifts of a person living outside by letting that person mentor your students for a day or a week. Remind your student that the true experts are those who carry the burden of whatever social oppression you are seeking to dismantle.

In the process, you can help the students you are mentoring abandon their comfort zone as you teach them to *practice immersion*. Communities look different from the sidewalk than from the window of an air-conditioned car. Learning how to share food with a person experiencing poverty is more important than hours volunteered in a food bank. Playing chess on a street corner can build trust. Porch sitting is real work and should be practiced often.

But porch sitting and deep listening and neighborhood lollygagging do not come naturally for our interns. In their short semesters with us, they are hoping to change the world (quickly) and learn enough while with us to get a world-changing job when they graduate. This is precisely why we must slow them down. If we don't insist on the slowness that cultivates community, they'll only learn to be saviors and colonizers.

IMAGINATION, STORYTELLING, AND CONNECTING

The work of mentoring is an apprenticeship without the how-to manual. Unlike a carpenter teaching a craft, we focus less on teaching logistics and try instead to *inspire imagination*. We know that context is everything, so we work by way of analogy. When we talk about a successful campaign, we remind our listeners that what works in one place cannot be replicated exactly in another. We deeply hope that what we teach and what students learn from people in our community will inspire enough imagination for them to dream up something completely different.

Storytelling is one way to inspire imaginative leaders. Stories help us connect with our neighbors and imagine what is possible. The stories we embrace and retell shape our relationality and open the possibility for social transformation. If the story I tell you about my neighborhood is one with "at-risk youth" and "failing schools," then I've painted a picture for you of a place where you do not want to live. In this story, the only roles you can imagine for yourself are victim or savior. If instead, I tell you a story about Ben, a high schooler who started a business fixing bikes for neighbors; or Pricilla, a local principal who cares more about students than test scores, then in this new story you will imagine something different. You'll bring your broken bike to Ben for a tune-up or volunteer with Pricilla to read to elementary school students. In stories where people and communities are not labeled as a means to our heroic ends, we can learn to live as neighbors, creating change together.

Yet storytelling, while deeply important, can also be dangerous. We know the dangers of telling an untrue story, but still another danger persists. My friend and colleague DeAmon Harges once said that when he is teaching people how to create change, he doesn't tell stories in fear that they might limit the imagination of his listeners. DeAmon coined the phrase "roving listener" to describe his work. He's a connector who constantly passes the mic to artists and entrepreneurs who are his neighbors. DeAmon and his neighbors have done some really amazing work creating transformation on the blocks that surround their houses, and everyone always wants to know exactly how this good work happened. But the way change happens in Indianapolis is not the same way change will come in Atlanta or Philly or Nairobi or Mexico City. Context and community are everything. As storytelling mentors, we must resist every urge to tell moralistic or prescriptive stories. Instead, we should teach those we mentor to practice deep listening as they hear the stories of their neighbors. In the process, we will all learn to tell a better story—a story that will catalyze change.

In this work of mentoring, we are not only storytellers, but also *connectors*. Our work is to introduce students to changemakers inside and outside our community. As we learn more about the gifts these students bring, we can connect them with other mentors who have similar or different gifts. We also connect students with texts that have shaped our work and contexts that have taught us new lessons. In some seasons of my work, I have taught students (much like the visitor to my office) who were hesitant to enter the fray of community work. I often described these students as needing permission to organize. In these times, I see myself as a connecter, taking scripture and putting it in dialogue with the lived experience of my neighbors, seeking to model a new way to live and work as a minister.

Sometimes the work of being a connector comes through the questions we ask. Our role as a mentor is too brief to ask boring questions. Good mentors think of questions that shift the ground underneath our feet. With these questions, the answers are less important than the seismic shift they require in the act of answering. My favorite question asker is Peter Block. He does this well in his book *Community: The Structure of Belonging*, but it is even more fun to be in a room with Peter when he's asking questions. He likes to put people in triads, force them to lean in where their knees are almost touching, and then ask the same question at least three times while never giving advice. Advice, according to Block, is a way of controlling others. The more difficult and important work is to listen without fixing, always responding with questions that force us to do our own work.

DOING OUR OWN WORK

This brings us to the final thing great mentors do . . . *they do their own work.* It is easy to give advice about how to not be racist or sexist or how not to colonize a community. It is harder to live into our own advice and do our own work. In mentoring, we must model success and failure. Our goal is not to fool those we mentor into thinking we are "woke" but to admit that each day brings new work we must do. As we name our own social location, we admit how this social location shapes us (with or without our permission). To do good work, we do not need to be perfect. When we mess up, we apologize. When we misstep, we listen to feedback. And just as we do not need to be perfect, we allow our students space to falter and fail. For sometimes failure is the greatest force to shape us into who we must become.

BUCKLE UP AND ENJOY THE RIDE

Mentoring is not rocket science. You won't do it perfectly, and in the end, all will still be well. Spacecraft will not fall out of the sky due to a slight mathematical error in your work, and for this we can give thanks to God. Like any work done in community, tending to relationships is essential to our success. If you're like me, you might think back on your mentoring experience and remember very little of the content and everything about the relationship. My seminary mentor was deeply formative in my life and is still a close friend to this day. This, in the end, is the greatest blessing of our work. The students we train will soon become our colleagues. If we do our job well, we will not create replicas of ourselves but inspire capable, amazing people who will listen to their own context and create their own change.

SUGGESTED READINGS AND RESOURCES

Adichie, Chimamanda Ngozi. *The Danger of a Single Story.* Ted Talk. https://www.ted.com/speakers/chimamanda_ngozi_adichie.
Block, Peter. *Community: The Structure of Belonging.* San Francisco: Berrett-Koehler, 2008.
Harges, DeAmon. *Making the Invisible Visible.* TEDx Indianapolis. https://tedxindianapolis.com/speakers/deamon-harges. See also https://thelearningtrees.com.
Isasi-Diaz, Ada Mariá. "Solidarity: Love of Neighbor in the Twenty-First Century." In *Mujerista Theology: A Theology for the Twenty-First Century.* New York: Orbis, 1996.
Mather, Michael. *Having Nothing, Possessing Everything: Finding Abundant Communities in Unexpected Places.* Grand Rapids, MI: Eerdmans, 2018.

Afterword

Supervision: Not an Afterthought

Matthew Floding

Supervision and mentoring are big jobs. They focus on the student's learning goals but keep the broad horizon of ministerial leadership in view at the same time. With this in mind, I brainstormed this list. As you think about your role in supervision and mentoring, you no doubt will expand on this.

Growth in character and spiritual formation:

- an authentic and maturing spirituality including sustaining spiritual practices, marked by growing love of God and love of persons
- appreciation of the particularities of place, its spiritual geography
- attentiveness and discernment
- authentic and integrated self, integrity
- courage to engage
- scriptural imagination
- theological integrity
- pastoral imagination when engaging (Aristotle's *phronesis* or practical wisdom), the capacity to do the right thing, for the right people, at the right time
- social awareness and empathy
- core values, ethics
- curiosity
- sacramental vision, wonder
- self-interrogation
- endurance and patience
- humility accompanied by an appropriate sense of an office's authority
- resources for resilience

Growth toward ministerial competency in:

- preaching
- teaching
- administration
- worship arts
- faith formation
- evangelism/mission
- caregiving
- advocacy/public theology
- inter-cultural humility
- leadership
- priestly sacramental presence
- systems thinking
- intersectional awareness
- imagination to innovate
- openness to collaborate
- professionalism to perform

It reminds me of Craig Dykstra's observation: "To be a good pastor, you have to be very smart in lots of interesting ways."[1]

We have used the term supervisor-mentor. The theological field educator you work with may feel the tension this hyphenated word captures.

When we entrust students to a field education site, we expect that they will be supervised appropriately. Roughly, that means supervisors negotiate learning goals, order the experience, provide accountability, make themselves accountable to the seminary or divinity school, support and evaluate the experience, and more. It is a role with a good deal of power. Evaluations sometimes factor into progress in the degree program through mid-program evaluations. Students often grant church judicatories and others access to evaluations as part of their credentialing or when applying for positions.

At the same time, we expect that they will be mentored. They are entering a community of practice after all, and they are becoming a kind of person, a ministerial leader. Mentors share ministerial life and stories, discern the Spirit's work, connect them to larger networks, coach for growth in competence, and reflect theologically with their mentees. It is a collegial role and one of mutual vulnerability. Jeremy Troxler captures this in his essay "Mentoring the Mother of God." Elizabeth has "been given three of the chief prerequisites for becoming a mentor: a life worthy of imitation, a wisdom worthy of being shared, and a character to which another's well-being can be trusted."[2]

In practice, as you know, these roles of supervisor and mentor are intertwined.

This book is dedicated to fostering transformative mentoring relationships. It happens best when both dimensions of supporting students are exercised. It's like jazz musician Wynton Marsalis's description of a musician exercising freedom within the form. "Anyone can improvise with no restrictions, but that's not jazz. Jazz always has some restrictions. Otherwise, it might sound like noise. The ability to improvise . . . comes from fundamental knowledge and this knowledge limits the choices you can make and will make."[3]

The effective supervisor-mentor attends to the details and the deadlines of the field education program. This is not glamorous work, but they are the "restrictions and the fundamental knowledge" that create the form in which your students can practice playing the scales of ministry. And, soon enough, growth through that discipline within the form will liberate the students to improvise in ministry, coupled with the knowledge that "jazz always has some restrictions."

We theological field educators have a front-row seat to observe your participation in the hard work and grace gift of ministerial formation. Students bear witness to the formational power of the relationship they have with you as their supervisor-mentor. Because evaluation documents are confidential, not often are you made aware of the enormity of the gift that you give. Students speak of a heightened sense of attentiveness to God at work forming them for their calling. Here are a few words of testimony:

> She is the kind of mentor that I wish everybody could learn from while discerning their vocation. She not only taught me what she has learned over the years but did so in the context of discerning my own gifts in a loving and open friendship. I am deeply grateful for her willingness to share her life with me.

> There is no limit to the number of pages it would require for me to fully express my love and respect for my supervisor-mentor. He models well what it means to live each moment in accordance with the Gospel; which challenged me to be more attentive to God at work in our church and the community—and in me! He has helped me become a better Christian.

> My placement has been a rollercoaster of experiences . . . [but] she is the light in the whole experience, and she, almost singlehandedly keeps me from becoming too jaded about organized religion and institutional church. I have found Jesus in abundance in my wonderful mentor.[4]

I think it only right, along with my colleagues who have contributed to this book, to express gratitude for the tireless effort that you make investing in the lives of students. I can't speak for you, but John Senior and I would like you and your colleagues in ministry to have the last word.

> Supervising and mentoring a student is like getting a bridge between past, present, and future—remembering the roots of my call, reflecting how and why I do ministry, and getting excited about those who will be leading the church in the future!

Mentoring a student is an opportunity every year, every season to put on fresh eyes; to see the church, calling, and ministry with freshness and newness—a beautiful reminder that God is always doing a new thing.

Supervising a student, to me, means indulging in the privilege of watching God at work in a disciple's life, and delighting in God's good gifts to the church through their life. [5]

Notes

INTRODUCTION

1. An excellent and recent resource in this regard is Dean K. Thompson and D. Cameron Murchison, eds., *Mentoring: Biblical, Theological, and Practical Perspectives* (Grand Rapids, MI: Eerdmans, 2018). Thompson and Murchison's volume explores mentoring in a wider frame than the present one, offering "windows on mentoring that are biblically grounded, theologically informed, communally diverse, and generationally attentive" (3). Another recent work, *Mentoring for Ministry: The Grace of Growing Pastors* (Eugene, OR: Cascade Books, 2017), edited by Craig T. Kocher, Jason Byassee, and James C. Howell, offers a variety of reflections on the work of mentoring for ministry by a group of authors whose lives and ministries have intersected in seminary, mentoring, and other professional experiences.

2. Pamela Holliman, "Mentoring as an Art of Intentional Thriving Together," 164, in *The Arts of Ministry: Feminist-Womanist Approaches*, edited by Christie Cozad Neuger (Louisville, KY: Westminster John Knox Press, 1996).

3. For a helpful contrast between expertise and wisdom as they relate to ministry, see Martin Copenhaver, "Expertise and Wisdom," 106–14, in *This Odd and Wondrous Calling: The Public and Private Lives of Two Ministers*, edited by Copenhaver and Lillian Daniel (Grand Rapids, MI: Eerdmans, 2000).

4. For useful discussions of the ways in which wisdom is embodied, see Christian Scharen, "Engaging the Intelligence of Practice," 1–22, in *Christian Practical Wisdom: What It Is, Why Is Matters*, edited by Dorothy C. Bass et al. (Grand Rapids, MI: Eerdmans, 2016). See also Craig Dykstra, "Pastoral and Ecclesial Imagination," 41–55, in *For Life Abundant: Practical Theology, Theological Education, and Christian Ministry*, edited by Dorothy C. Bass and Craig Dykstra (Grand Rapids, MI: Eerdmans, 2008).

5. Parker J. Palmer, *Let Your Life Speak: Listening to the Voice of Vocation* (San Francisco: Jossey-Bass, 2001), 11.

6. Barbara Blodgett explores another layer of this balance between structure and openness in her book *Becoming the Pastor You Hope to Be*. Blodgett distinguishes between what she calls "functionalist" and "transformative" mentoring. Functionalist mentoring focuses on "learning the ropes," becoming proficient in the skills and practices of work relevant in a particular context. The traditions, histories, practices, and so on that give shape to any context of ministry render intelligible what "proficiency" means in that setting. Transformative mentoring, by contrast, calls the mentee's attention to questions about the context itself: why are things the way they are, and how might things be done differently? Good leaders, Blodgett is

saying, are both skillful practitioners in the ways their context demands and also continually ask questions about how the context itself is evolving.

7. We considered adding to this section chapters on mentoring persons who inhabit different cultural and ethnic identities. The recent volume edited by Thompson and Murchison, *Mentoring: Biblical, Theological, and Practical Perspectives* (cited above), offers excellent chapters that explore mentoring persons who inhabit African American, Roman Catholic, Latin@, and East Asian identities. We did not feel the need to duplicate the good work done in *Mentoring* here. We did, however, include a couple of chapters on mentoring around identities that *Mentoring* does not address directly.

1. MENTORING ETHICALLY

1. Barbara Blodgett, "Ministerial Ethics," 115, in *Welcome to Theological Field Education!*, edited by Matthew Floding (Herndon, VA: Alban Institute, 2011).

2. Richard Gula, *Ethics in Pastoral Ministry* (Mahwah, NJ: Paulist Press, 1996), 3.

3. Blodgett, "Ministerial Ethics," 116–17.

4. Seminaries and divinity schools have different names for this formal learning agreement.

5. "Most of what is learned and taught is not quantifiable. Articulating the content of this interaction is often difficult because formation relies less on content and more on the context of the learning: the relationship." Charlene Jin Lee, "The Art of Supervision and Formation," 18–19, in *Welcome to Theological Field Education!*, edited by Matthew Floding (Herndon, VA: Alban Institute, 2011).

6. See Richard Gula's *Ethics in Pastoral Ministry*; Joseph Bush's *Gentle Shepherding*; and Walter Wiest and Elwyn Smith's *Ethics in Ministry* for thorough discussions on confidentiality.

7. Barbara Blodgett, "Engaging in Ministry Ethically," 29, in *Engage: A Theological Field Education Toolkit*, edited by Matthew Floding (Lanham, MD: Rowman & Littlefield, 2017).

2. MENTORING FOR VOCATIONAL DISCERNMENT

1. A classic guide to committees for clearness is Jan Hoffman's "Clearness Committees and Their Use in Personal Discernment," accessed April 20, 2019, http://atlantaquakers.org/_site_pdf_docs/clearness_committees_and_their_use.

2. Patricia Loring, *Spiritual Discernment: The Context and Goal of Clearness Committees* (Wallingford, PA: Pendle Hill, 1992), 19–21.

3. http://www.couragerenewal.org/approach/, accessed May 5, 2019.

4. Ken Medema, "Teach Me to Stop and Listen," accessed April 20, 2019, https://www.youtube.com/watch?v=uJgteoznY28; words and music are in *Worship in Song: A Friends Hymnal* (Philadelphia: Friends General Conference, 1996), #137.

5. Cynthia Bourgeaux, *Centering Prayer and Inner Awakening* (Lanham, MD: Cowley, 2004), 4–6.

6. "The Steps of Lectio Divina," accessed April 20, 2019, https://www.conceptionabbey.org/wpcontent/uploads/2018/11/lectio-divina-card.pdf.

7. Such as "Nada te turbe/Nothing Can Trouble," words and music in Jacques Berthier, *Songs & Prayers from Taizé, Basic Edition* (Taizé: Les Presses de Taizé, 1991), 50.

8. Such as Melanie Weidner's "The knowing blooms when I am still," accessed April 20, 2019, https://www.listenforjoy.com/1990/01/01/knowing-blooms/.

9. Margaret Fell (1694), quoted in London Yearly Meeting, *Christian Faith and Practice in the Experience of the Society of Friends* (Richmond, IN: Friends United Press, 1973), Selection 20.

10. Patricia Loring, *Spiritual Discernment: The Context and Goal of Clearness Committees* (Wallingford, PA: Pendle Hill, 1985), 24.

11. Parker Palmer, *Let Your Life Speak: Listening for the Voice of Vocation* (San Francisco, CA: Jossey-Bass, 2000), 7–8.

12. https://onbeing.org/programs/ruby-sales-where-does-it-hurt-aug2017/, accessed May 5, 2019.

13. Suzanne Farnham et al., *Listening Hearts; Discerning Call in Community* (Harrisburg, PA: Morehouse Publishing, 2011), 24, quoting John S. Dunne, *The Way of All the Earth: Experiments in Truth and Religion* (Notre Dame, IN: University of Notre Dame Press, 1972), 39.

14. Jan Wood, "Spiritual Discernment: The Personal Dimension," Friends Consultation on Discernment (Richmond, IN: Quaker Hill Conference Center, 1985), 8.

15. Susan Stark, "Live Up to the Light," accessed April 26, 2019, https://www.youtube.com/watch?v=c603RMLaR0o.

16. Palmer, *Let Your Life Speak*, 54.

3. MENTORING FOR SPIRITUAL DEVELOPMENT

1. Galatians 5:25.

2. If you must have compliance regarding a particular ministry activity, be curious as to why. If it is because you are their supervisor and need a particular action from your mentees, express it that way.

3. John 4:26.

4. https://www.crcna.org/welcome/beliefs/confessions/heidelberg-catechism, Heidelberg Catechism, Q&A 53, accessed March 18, 2019.

4. MENTORING FOR HEALTHY BOUNDARY MAKING AND BOUNDARY KEEPING

1. Howard Thurman, "The Sound of the Genuine," *The Spelman Messenger* 96 (Summer 1980).

2. Thurman, "Sound of the Genuine," 14–15.

5. MENTORING FOR LIFE-GIVING RELATIONSHIPS

1. Terry Parsons, PhD clinical psychology, who works with the Perkins Intern Program advising mentor pastors and students on internship. This is advice he gives to both every year.

2. Flora Slosson Wuellner, *Prayer, Stress, and Our Inner Wounds* (Nashville: Upper Room, 1995), 16.

3. Mark 9:7.

4. Wendell Berry, "The Peace of Wild Things," https://onbeing.org/poetry/the-peace-of-wild-things/, accessed May 28, 2019.

5. Henri, J. M. Nouwen, *In the Name of Jesus: Reflections of Christian Leadership* (New York: Crossroad, 1996), 50.

6. Wuellner, *Prayer, Stress, and Our Inner Wounds*, 15.

7. Nouwen, *In the Name of Jesus*, 42.

8. Wuellner, *Prayer, Stress, and Our Inner Wounds*, 87.

9. Wuellner, *Prayer, Stress, and Our Inner Wounds*, 88.

10. Wuellner, *Prayer, Stress, and Our Inner Wounds*, 89.

11. Wuellner, *Prayer, Stress, and Our Inner Wounds*, 90–91.

12. Wuellner, *Prayer, Stress, and Our Inner Wounds*, 92–93.

13. Nouwen, *In the Name of Jesus*, 71–72.

14. https://www.therapistaid.com/worksheets/self-care-assessment.pdf, accessed May 30, 2019.

6. MENTORING FOR PASTORAL IMAGINATION

1. Names have been changed to preserve confidentiality.

2. I am grateful for my colleagues on the Pastoral Imagination research team, Codirector Christian Scharen and Associate Director Catrina Ciccone, who both offered insight and feedback on this chapter. "Naomi" is a pseudonym, and this chapter is based on stories she has conveyed to us since 2009.

3. Craig Dykstra, "Pastoral and Ecclesial Imagination," 41–61, in *For Life Abundant: Practical Theology, Theological Education, and Christian Ministry*, edited by Dorothy C. Bass and Craig Dykstra (Grand Rapids, MI: Eerdmans, 2008).

4. This is one of six key findings in the Five-Year Report. See Christian A. B. Scharen and Eileen R. Campbell-Reed, *The Learning Pastoral Imagination Project: A Five-Year Report on How New Ministers Learn in Practice* (New York: Auburn Studies, no. 21 [Winter 2016]).

5. A helpful site for understanding consensus decision making is https://www.seedsforchange.org.uk/consensus.

6. Within the consensus model, "standing aside" is a form of refusal to take part in a decision that the majority is moving to adopt.

7. Eileen Campbell-Reed and Christian Scharen, "Ministry as Spiritual Practice: How Pastors Learn to See and Respond to the 'More' of a Situation," *Journal of Religious Leadership* 12, no. 2 (2013).

7. MENTORING FOR RESILIENCE

1. Grateful thanks to Dr. Katherine A. for her many years of thoughtful care.

2. "Flourishing in Ministry: Emerging Research Insights on the Well-Being of Pastors," Notre Dame, IN: University of Notre Dame, 2013, https://workwellresearch.com/media/images/Emerging%20Insights.pdf, 20–21.

3. "Flourishing in Ministry," 20.

8. MENTORING FOR THEOLOGICAL REFLECTION

1. Brené Brown, *Daring Greatly* (New York: Avery, 2012), 46.

2. https://www.ignatianspirituality.com/ignatian-prayer/the-examen, accessed January 3, 2019.

3. "If theology is to matter, it, like Jesus, must 'become flesh and dwell among us'" (John 1:14). Theological field education (TFE), this report will show, is a powerfully generative mode for theology to become flesh and dwell among us, thereby making theology matter, and matter for the same end to which the incarnation itself was directed: 'the world' (John 3:16)." Christian Scharen and Sharon Miller, "Making Theology Matter," Auburn Seminary Report, August 2018, https://auburnseminary.org/report/making-theology-matter/, accessed December 31, 2018.

4. Ada Maria Isasi-Diaz, *In La Lucha /In the Struggle: Elaboration of a Mujerista Theology* (Minneapolis, MN: Augsburg Fortress, 2004). Three examples of how using the alternative "Kin-dom of God" is helpful (English language translation of "Familia de Dios" by theologian Isasi-Díaz). First, from the 2018 PCUSA General Assembly Bible Study: "The kin-dom of God is built not through competition but in mutual cooperation and solidarity. People who are part of kin-dom use their resources and privilege to advocate for others who are less privileged." https://www.pcusa.org/news/2018/2/12/bible-study-ga223-will-explore-kin-dom-versus-king/ accessed December 29, 2018. Second, from Pastor Melissa Florer-Bixler writing in Sojourners on November 20, 2018, "In the 37 times that Jesus describes the reign of God in the Gospels, not once is the kingdom of God like a kingdom of earth." https://sojo.net/articles/kin-dom-christ accessed 12/28/2018. Third, Jesus too spoke of a Kingdom kinship, "For whoever does the will of my Father in heaven is my brother and sister and mother" (Matthew 12:49). A colleague and I have offered this working definition of theological reflection in field education as "reflection upon lived, embodied experiences in ministry that seeks to make sense of practice and form reflectors in habits for competent ministry." Barbara Blodgett and Matthew Floding, *Brimming with God: Reflecting Theologically on Cases in Ministry* (Eugene, OR: Wipf and Stock, 2015), 4.

5. A colleague and I have offered this working definition of theological reflection in field education as "reflection upon lived, embodied experiences in ministry that seeks to make sense of practice and form reflectors in habits for competent ministry." Barbara Blodgett and Matthew Floding, *Brimming with God: Reflecting Theologically on Cases in Ministry* (Eugene, OR: Wipf and Stock, 2015), 4.

6. Craig Dykstra, "Pastoral and Ecclesial Imagination," 47, in Dorothy Bass and Craig Dykstra, eds., *For Life Abundant* (Grand Rapids, MI: Eerdmans, 2008).

7. Howard W. Stone and James O. Duke, *How to Think Theologically*, 3rd ed. (Minneapolis, MN: Fortress, 2013), 18.

8. Adapted from Barbara Blodgett and Matthew Floding, *Brimming with God*, chapter 2.

9. Names have been altered to preserve confidentiality and excerpts are used with permission.

9. MENTORING FOR CULTURAL HUMILITY

1. For the "Cultural Competency" and "The Journey toward Cultural Humility" sections, I used and adapted sections of three of my published articles with Sojourners, Christian Century, and Faith and Leadership.

2. Miguel Gallardo, *Developing Cultural Humility: Embracing Race, Privilege and Power* (Los Angeles: Sage, 2014), 219.

3. Tervalon, Melanie, and Jann Murray-García, "Cultural Humility Versus Cultural Competence: A Critical Distinction in Defining Physician Training Outcomes in Multicultural Education," *Journal of Health Care for the Poor and Underserved* 9, no. 2 (1998): 117–25.

4. Tervalon and Murray-García, "Cultural Humility Versus Cultural Competence."

5. People involved in the stories have granted permission to use their stories; however, the names were changed to protect their identity and privacy.

6. This is what I call an awareness tool because it measures the readiness and openness of people to interact with other cultures; more information about the tool can be found at https://idiinventory.com/.

11. MENTORING FOR RELATIONAL CONFLICT

1. https://ditl.wordpress.com/2011/07/24/christian-conflict-management/, accessed August 1, 2019.

12. MENTORING WITH GENDER IN MINDBODYSPIRIT

1. I am grateful to the students who were generous in allowing the use of their stories in this chapter.

2. "Definitions Related to Sexual Orientation and Gender Diversity in APA Documents," 2012, https://www.apa.org/pi/lgbt/resources/sexuality-definitions.pdf.

3. Mahzarin Banaji and Anthony Greenwald, *Blindspot: Hidden Biases of Good People* (New York: Delacourte, 2013).

4. Although I write from my own religious tradition, I encourage each of us to consider our own traditions' resources.

5. A. D. "Flanny" Flanigan, Project 360, April 4, 2019.

6. M. Shawn Copeland, *Enfleshing Freedom: Body, Race, and Being* (Minneapolis, MN: Fortress Press, 2010), 24.

7. Abbey Labrecque, Project 360, April 6, 2019.

8. Mayra Rivera, "Carnal Corporeality: Tensions in Continental and Caribbean Thought," mayrarivera.com/files/mayrarivera/files/carnal_corporeality-concordia.pdf.

9. Summer Hyche, Project 360, April 4, 2019.

10. Michael Kimmel and Lisa Wade, "Ask a Feminist: Michael Kimmel and Lisa Wade Discuss Toxic Masculinities," *University of Chicago Press Journals: Signs, Journal of Women in Culture and Society* 44, no. 1 (Autumn 2018), https://www.journals.uchicago.edu/doi/full/10.1086/698284. It is not within the scope of this chapter to explore the particularity of expressions of toxic masculinities across racial/ethnic identities. I include whiteness as a racial identity.

11. Mollie Donihe, Project 360, April 4, 2019.

12. A former student wrote these aspects of being human in one word as a way of claiming a holistic theological anthropology. I am grateful for this creative insight.

13. Text message, Kelsey Davis, April 18, 2019.

14. Rhea Miller, *Cloudhand Clenched Fist* (Philadelphia: Innisfree Press, 1996), 31.

15. Parker Palmer, "Withering into the Truth," February 22, 2017, https://onbeing.org/blog/withering-into-the-truth/.

16. Kelsey Davis, senior project, 2018.

17. Summer Hyche, Project 360, April 4, 2019.

18. Phone conversation with Kelsey Davis, April 18, 2019. Source: Martin B Copenhaver, *Jesus is the Question* (Nashville: Abingdon Press, 2014).

19. Traci C. West examines how "a broader, collective and communal process supports . . . heterosexist and male entitlements." Traci C. West, *Disruptive Christian Ethics: When Racism and Women's Lives Matter* (Louisville, KY: Westminster John Knox Press, 2006), 66.

20. Although this reflection references "church," I invite you to consider its relevance for multiple faith settings.

21. Brent Roe-Hall, case study, February 2019.

13. MENTORING LGBTQIA STUDENTS

1. Lesbian, Gay, Bisexual, Transgender, Queer, Intersex, and Asexual. At times in the chapter I will use the term "queer" as an identifier that encompasses sexual/affectional orientations and gender identities beyond straight and cisgender ones, but that shouldn't be seen to mask the pluriformity of embodiments that exist under the moniker of "queer."

2. Affectional orientation is often used alongside or in place of sexual orientation to indicate that "sexual" attraction is only one factor in a person's sense of attraction to another person, highlighting the emotional components and desires for connection that are an important part in a person's sense of romantic attraction to another person.

3. People whose gender as assigned at birth matches their bodily presentation of gender and their own psychological and spiritual sense of gender identity.

4. For more on microaggressions, see Cody J. Sanders and Angela Yarber, *Microaggressions in Ministry: Confronting the Hidden Violence of Everyday Church* (Louisville, KY: Westminster John Knox, 2015).

5. Darnell L. Moore, "Coming Out or Inviting In?: Part I," *Feminist Wire* (July 12, 2012), accessed online at http://www.thefeministwire.com/2012/07/coming-out-or-inviting-in-reframing-disclosure-paradigms-part-i/.

6. Darnell L. Moore, "Coming Out or Inviting In?: Part II," *Feminist Wire* (July 13, 2012), accessed online at: http://www.thefeministwire.com/2012/07/coming-out-or-inviting-in-part-ii/
.

7. Joretta L. Marshall, "Differences, Dialogues, and Discourses: From Sexuality to Queer Theory in Learning and Teaching," *Journal of Pastoral Theology* 19, no. 2 (2009): 29.

8. Marshall, "Differences, Dialogues, and Discourses," 39.

9. Cody J. Sanders, *Queer Lessons for Churches on the Straight and Narrow: What All Christians Can Learn from LGBTQ Lives* (Macon, GA: Faithlab, 2013).

14. TRAUMA-INFORMED MENTORING

1. National Council for Behavioral Health, "How to Manage Trauma," https://www.thenationalcouncil.org/wp-content/uploads/2013/05/Trauma-infographic.pdf.

2. Peter A. Levine, *Waking the Tiger: Healing Trauma* (Berkeley, CA: North Atlantic Books, 1997), 28.

3. Bessel Van Der Kolk, *The Body Keeps the Score: Brain, Mind, and the Body in the Healing of Trauma* (New York: Penguin, 2014), 1–2.

4. Resmaa Menakem, *My Grandmother's Hands: Racialized Trauma and the Pathway to Mending Our Hearts and Bodies* (Las Vegas, NV: Central Recovery Press, 2017), 165.

5. Denise E. Elliott, Paula Bjelajac, Roger D. Fallot, Laurie S. Markoff, and Beth Lover Reed, "Trauma-informed or Trauma-denied: Principles and Implementation of Trauma-Informed Services for Women," *Journal of Community Psychology* 33, no. 4 (2005): 461–77, https://www.mappingthemaze.org.uk/wp-content/uploads/2017/08/Trauma-Informed-Care-Services-for-Women.pdf.

15. MENTORING FOR LEADERSHIP IN NONPROFIT SETTINGS

1. Cynthia Moe-Lobeda, *Resisting Structural Evil: Love as Ecological-Economic Vocation* (Minneapolis, MN: Fortress Press, 2013), 12.

2. See the essays in INCITE!, *The Revolution Will Not Be Funded: Beyond the Nonprofit Industrial Complex* (Durham, NC: Duke University Press, 2017).

3. Lester M. Salomon, "The Nonprofitization of the Welfare State," *Voluntas* 26 (2015): 2147–54.

16. MENTORING FOR MINISTRY IN CHAPLAINCY SETTINGS

1. Names have been changed throughout to preserve confidentiality.

2. https://www.youtube.com/watch?v=1Evwgu369Jw.

3. http://blog.newmediaprojectatunion.org/2011/08/ministry-of-presence.html.

4. Henri Nouwen, *Out of Solitude: Three Meditations on the Christian Life* (Notre Dame, IN: Ave Maria Press, 1974), 38.

5. Nicholas Wolterstorff, *Lament for a Son* (Grand Rapids, MI: Eerdmans, 1987), 34.

17. MENTORING IN ONLINE MEDIA

1. http://www.darktable.ca/about.html.

18. THE CONGREGATION AS MENTOR

1. This liturgy for infant baptism comes from the Reformed Church in America. For those practicing believers' baptism, it may be helpful to frame this within the Church's commitment to disciple and empower for ministry all baptized believers.

2. Laurent Parks Daloz, Cheryl Keen, James Keen, and Sharon Daloz Parks, *Common Fire: Leading Lives of Commitment in a Complex World* (Boston: Beacon, 1996).

3. Samuel Wells, *Improvisation: The Drama of Christian Ethics* (Grand Rapids, MI: Brazos, 2004), 44.

4. Statements from Duke Divinity School students evaluating their placements, edited to preserve confidentiality and used with permission.

19. MENTORING BEYOND SEMINARY

1. From a September 2018 phone conversation with a denominational leader.

2. From a June 2011 feedback session with a group of mentees.

3. From a story shared by a colleague in a May 2013 meeting.

20. MENTORING FOR COURAGEOUS LEADERSHIP

1. William Stafford, *Crossing Unmarked Snow* (Ann Arbor: University of Michigan Press, 1998), 29.

2. Names have been changed to preserve confidentiality.

21. MENTORING THE PREACHER

1. Kathleen Cahalan, presentation at the Association of Theological Field Educators Biennial Meeting, January 2017.

22. MENTORING THE ADMINISTRATOR

1. Becky R. McMillan, "What Do Clergy Do All Week?" Pulpit & Pew: Research on Pastoral Leadership. Accessed February 14, 2019, http://pulpitandpew.org/node/823.

2. "The pastors of America have metamorphosed into a company of shopkeepers, and the shops they keep are churches." Eugene H. Peterson, *Working the Angles: The Shape of Pastoral Integrity* (Grand Rapids, MI: Eerdmans, 1987), 2.

3. "The basic work of any Christian ministry is to preach the gospel of Jesus Christ in the power of God's Spirit, and to see people converted, changed, and grow to maturity in that gospel. That's the work of planting, watering, fertilizing and tending the vine. However, just as some sort of framework is needed to help a vine grow, so Christian ministries also need some structure and support. And that's the thing about trellis work: it tends to take over from vine work." Colin Marshall and Tony Payne, *The Trellis and the Vine: The Ministry Mind-Shift That Changes Everything* (Kingsford, Australia: Matthias Media, 2009), 8–9.

23. MENTORING THE PASTORAL CAREGIVER

1. Jeanne Stevenson-Moessner, *A Primer in Pastoral Care* (Minneapolis, MN: Augsburg Fortress, 2005).

24. MENTORING FOR FAITH FORMATION

1. Karl Barth, "The Strange New World within the Bible," in *The Word of God and the Word of Man*, edited and translated by Douglas Horton (Boston: Pilgrim, 1928), 28 (my emphasis), 44, 43. The original German title of Barth's famous address that was delivered in the church of Leutwil, Switzerland, on February 6, 1917, at the invitation of its pastor and his friend Edward Thurneysen was simply "Die neue Welt in der Bibel (The New World within the Bible)."

2. Brady Bryce, "Stumbling into Theological Field Education: Exploring the Move from 'Knowing How' to 'Teaching How,'" in *Reflective Practice: Formation and Supervision in Ministry* 38 (2018): 231, 237. "Success in 'knowing how' to do ministry," concludes Bryce, "does not directly mean success in 'teaching how' ministers serve. The wisdom and resources of people who have traveled this path [of theological field education] are worthy of our attentive listening" (240).

3. Charlene Jin Lee, "The Art of Supervision and Formation," in *Welcome to Theological Field Education!*, ed. Matthew Floding (Herndon, VA: Alban, 2011), 21, 24 (original emphasis), 26, 27.

4. Sung Hee Chang, "Engaging in Faith Formation," 80–81, in *Engage: A Theological Field Education Toolkit*, edited by Matthew Floding (Lanham, MD: Rowman & Littlefield, 2017). "First, *it is God who ultimately forms faith.*" "Second, *faith formation takes the experience of context seriously.*" "Third, *it takes a whole congregation to form faith.*" "Fourth, *faith formation is not a program but a process.*"

5. Philip Yancey, *Soul Survivor: How Thirteen Unlikely Mentors Helped My Faith Survive the Church* (New York: Doubleday, 2003), 10.

6. Leona M. English, *Mentoring in Religious Education* (Birmingham, AL: Religious Education Press, 1998), 88. As English puts it, mentoring is "a means of living one's vocation" (footnote 29).

7. Walter Brueggemann, "Mentoring in the Old Testament," 9, in *Mentoring: Biblical, Theological, and Practical Perspectives*, edited by Dean K. Thompson and D. Cameron Mur-

chison (Grand Rapids, MI: Eerdmans, 2018). Here Brueggemann sees the book of Job as an exception to this "one-directional" wisdom tradition.

8. David L. Bartlett, "Mentoring in the New Testament," 36 (my emphasis), in *Mentoring: Biblical, Theological, and Practical Perspectives*, edited by Dean K. Thompson and D. Cameron Murchison (Grand Rapids, MI: Eerdmans, 2018).

9. Cynthia L. Rigby, "Expanding the Perimeters of Feminist Mentoring," 88, in *Mentoring: Biblical, Theological, and Practical Perspectives*, edited by Dean K. Thompson and D. Cameron Murchison (Grand Rapids, MI: Eerdmans, 2018).

10. Thomas W. Currie III, "Theological-Pastoral Perspectives on Mentoring," 40, in *Mentoring: Biblical, Theological, and Practical Perspectives*, edited by Dean K. Thompson and D. Cameron Murchison (Grand Rapids, MI: Eerdmans, 2018). It does not negate the mentor's role of guiding the common journey. "Mentors seem to do three fairly distinct things: they *support*, they *challenge*, and they *provide vision*. . . . By their very existence, mentors provide proof that the journey can be made, the leap taken." Laurent A. Daloz, *Mentor: Guiding the Journey of Adult Learners* (San Francisco: Jossey-Bass, 1999), 206–7 (original emphasis).

11. Luke Timothy Johnson, "Mentoring in the Roman Catholic Tradition," 136, 138, in *Mentoring: Biblical, Theological, and Practical Perspectives*, edited by Dean K. Thompson and D. Cameron Murchison (Grand Rapids, MI: Eerdmans, 2018).

12. Douglas Ottati and Elizabeth Hinson-Hasty, "Mentoring toward a Humane Disposition, Attitude, and Imagination," 199, in *Mentoring: Biblical, Theological, and Practical Perspectives*, edited by Dean K. Thompson and D. Cameron Murchison (Grand Rapids, MI: Eerdmans, 2018). Ottati and Hinson-Hasty promote "a broader and deeper idea of mentoring" toward "a humane disposition, attitude, and imagination in the midst of the many roles and demands of life together" (198, 207).

13. Thomas W. Currie III, *The Joy of Ministry* (Louisville, KY: Westminster John Knox, 2008), 2. The following is the basic argument of Currie: "We have grown busy but not joyful." The problem of joylessness in ministry should be addressed squarely and "the recovery of the gospel's gift of joy" attempted soundly. For God created all God's creatures for "participating in their own way in the joy of knowing God" and "in the joy of God's own life." "[I]t is the gospel's joy that enables us to love ministry, to give ourselves to it, and even more important, to love those with whom we minister" (5, 3, 38, 101).

14. Currie, *The Joy of Ministry*, 47.

15. Rita Dunn, Jeffrey S. Beaudry, and Angela Klavas, "Survey of Research on Learning Styles." *California Journal of Science Education* 2, no. 2 (Spring 2002): 75, 88 (original emphasis). The theme of this issue of the journal is "What We Know about How People Learn."

16. Henri J. M. Nouwen, *The Genesee Diary: Report from a Trappist Monastery*, complete and unabridged (New York: Doubleday, 1981 [1976]), 217.

17. See Kathleen A. Cahalan, "Callings over a Lifetime: In Relationship, through the Body, over Time, and for Community," in *Calling All Years Good: Christian Vocation throughout Life's Seasons*, edited by Kathleen A. Cahalan and Miller-McLemore. Cahalan's summary of the lifelong/life span perspective is this: "callings are discerned through relationships; they evolve over time; they are multiple and changing; they are dependent on the emergent capacities of the body; and, last but not least, they are mutually influencing and responsive to others" (13).

18. Angela H. Reed, Richard A. Osmer, and Marcus G. Smucker, *Spiritual Companioning: A Guide to Protestant Theology and Practice* (Grand Rapids, MI: Baker Academic, 2015), 141.

19. Will Willimon, "The Gifts of Mentors in Ministry," in *Mentoring for Ministry: The Grace of Growing Pastors*, edited by Craig T. Kocher, Jason Byassee, and James C. Howell (Eugene, OR: Cascade, 2017), 49.

20. To help you and your mentee to unlearn, you may draw on, among many critical learning theorists, Katie Cannon's womanist mentoring work that has "three separate but intertwined movements: (1) *debunking* the matrix of power, (2) *unmasking* the pedagogy of the opposable thumb, and (3) *disentangling* deliberate distortions in biblical hermeneutics [and theological theories]." Katie Geneva Cannon, "Womanist Mentoring—African American Perspectives," 124 (original emphasis), in *Mentoring: Biblical, Theological, and Practical Per-*

spectives, edited by Dean K. Thompson and D. Cameron Murchison (Grand Rapids, MI: Eerdmans, 2018).

21. Eric H. F. Law, *Inclusion: Making Room for Grace* (St. Louis, MO: Chalice, 2000), 43, 103.

AFTERWORD. SUPERVISION: NOT AN AFTERTHOUGHT

1. Craig Dykstra, "Pastoral and Ecclesial Imagination," 51, in *For Life Abundant*, edited by Dorothy Bass and Craig Dykstra (Grand Rapids, MI: Eerdmans, 2008).

2. Jeremy Troxler, "Mentoring the Mother of God," 2, in *Mentoring for Ministry: The Grace of Growing Pastors*, edited by Craig T. Kocher, Jason Byassee, and James Howell (Eugene, OR: Cascade, 2017).

3. Wynton Marsalis cited in *Community Building: Freedom Within Form*, https://www.instructionalcoaching.com/downloads/pdfs/HII_MM_FreedomWithinForm.pdf, accessed December 14, 2018.

4. Comments taken from student evaluation forms.

5. Comments taken from a survey conducted among Duke Divinity School supervisor-mentors in August 2018.

Index

About the Contributors

Rev. Catherine M. Brall, DMin, formerly served as director of field education at Pittsburgh Theological Seminary. She currently serves as priest at St. Thomas Episcopal Church in Canonsburg, Pennsylvania.

Rev. Melissa Browning, PhD, is interim director of contextual education and international partnerships at Columbia Theological Seminary in Decatur, Georgia. Melissa is a theologian, ethicist, and activist who studies community-based responses to injustice. For more about Melissa's work, visit www.melissabrowning.com.

Rev. Eileen R. Campbell-Reed, PhD, is coordinator of coaching, mentoring, and internships at Central Seminary (Tennessee campus). Currently she is visiting associate professor of pastoral theology and care at Union Theological Seminary, New York City. She is codirector of the Learning Pastoral Imagination Project, host of Three Minute Ministry Mentor, and author of *State of Clergywomen in the US* (2018) and *Anatomy of a Schism* (2016).

Rev. Amy Canosa, MDiv, is an ACPE certified educator at Duke Raleigh Hospital in Raleigh, North Carolina. She is an ordained Baptist minister and is endorsed through the Alliance of Baptists.

Sung Hee Chang is director of the Asian American Ministry Center and assistant professor of Christian education at Union Presbyterian Seminary. Previously, she had served as an educator in several churches in Virginia and North Carolina. Her areas of special interest include curriculum theory with particular attention to gender, race, identity, and postcolonial studies, intercultural theological education, ecumenical formation, interreligious education, and Asian theological education. She currently serves on the Presbyterian Church (USA) Educator Certification Committee.

Rev. Jill Y. Crainshaw, PhD, is Blackburn Professor of Worship and Liturgical Theology at Wake Forest University School of Divinity in Winston-Salem, North Carolina, where she also serves as vice dean of faculty development and academic initiatives. She is the author of several books, including *When I in Awesome Wonder: Liturgy Distilled from Everyday Life* (2018).

Stephanie Crumley-Effinger, director of supervised ministry at Earlham school of religion, is a recorded minister in the Religious Society of Friends (Quakers). She has been in her current position since 2000 following eighteen years directing campus and Quaker ministries, first at Wilmington College of Ohio and then at Earlham College. Although Stephanie occasionally has had a chapter published in an edited compilation, her main body of writing is feedback on student assignments, previously written in purple ink and currently in purple type, seeking to nurture the students' spiritual, intellectual, and professional growth through her input.

Rev. Dr. Isabel N. Docampo is on the faculty at Perkins School of Theology of Southern Methodist University where she is codirector of the intern program and director of The Center for the Study of Latino/a Christianity and Religions. She is an ordained American Baptist Churches USA clergywoman. She contributed a chapter to *Brimming with God*.

Margaret Elliott is executive director of Crisis Control Ministry in Winston-Salem, North Carolina. She is responsible for the overall operations of the ministry as well as community relations, board relations, fund-raising, and strategic planning. Margaret has a BA in political science from St. Andrews Presbyterian College and a master's in public administration from the University of North Carolina at Greensboro. She is an ordained ruling elder with the Presbyterian Church (USA), serves as clerk of session at Trinity Presbyterian Church, and serves on the coordinating committees of several collaborative groups.

Matthew Floding is director of ministerial formation at Duke Divinity School. He has served as a theological field educator since 1999 following service as pastor and college chaplain. He is editor and contributor to *Welcome to Theological Field Education!*, *Engage: A Theological Field Education Toolkit*, and, coeditor and contributor to *Enlighten: Formational Learning in Theological Field Education*. He is coeditor of the journal *Reflective*

Practice: Formation and Supervision in Ministry and is past chair of the Association for Theological Field Education.

Thomas L. Fuller is associate dean at Beeson Divinity School, Samford University, in Birmingham, Alabama. For two decades he taught courses in pastoral leadership and directed Beeson's theological field education program. He has served as pastor to several churches in Alabama and Indiana. Tom contributed chapters to *Preparing for Ministry* (2008) and *Brimming with God* (2015).

Rev. Dr. Tracy Hartman, PhD, most recently served as the Daniel O. Aleshire Professor of Homiletics and Practical Theology at Baptist Theological Seminary in Richmond, Virginia, where she also served as vice president of academic affairs and dean. She just concluded a term as chair of the Association of Theological Field Educators. She is the author of *Letting the Other Speak: Proclaiming the Stories of Biblical Women* and coauthor of *New Proclamation Commentary*. She also contributed to the *Feasting on the Word* and *Feasting on the Gospels* commentary series.

Margrethe Floding Jasker, MS, is a patient relations specialist in Portland, Oregon. She earned her master of science in conflict resolution from Portland State University. She grew up as a pastor's daughter and has served on the staff at First Presbyterian Church, Portland. Prior to working in the area of conflict resolution, she practiced social work in Chicago and Michigan. She was also a member of the Conflict Resolution Resource Center, a group that designed conflict resolution training programs.

William B. Kincaid is Herald B. Monroe Professor of Leadership and Ministry Studies at Christian Theological Seminary in Indianapolis, Indiana, where he also directs the transition into ministry initiative The First Season Project. He is the author of *Finding Voice: How Theological Field Education Shapes Pastoral Identity* and *Like Stepping into a Canoe: Nimbleness and the Transition into Ministry*.

Nathan E. Kirkpatrick is managing director of Alban at Duke Divinity School in Durham, North Carolina. In this role, he designs educational programs, facilitates leadership development opportunities for clergy, denominational and institutional leaders, works with publisher Rowman & Littlefield to publish Alban books, and consults with senior church leaders around the United States and abroad. He has degrees from Wake Forest University and Duke University Divinity School. He is a priest in the Episcopal Church and serves as priest associate at The Church of the Advocate in Chapel Hill.

Rev. Susan L. LeFeber, DMin, is director of seminary vocation, director of field education and placement, and assistant professor of ministry at the University of Dubuque Theological Seminary. She has published articles in *Reflective Practice* and *The International Congregational Journal*.

Rev. Dr. Susan MacAlpine-Gillis is assistant professor of pastoral theology at Atlantic School of Theology in Halifax, Nova Scotia, where she teaches supervised field education for on-campus students and works with students across the country enrolled in AST's distance MDiv. Ordained by the United Church of Canada in 1985, Susan enjoyed thirty-one years of congregational ministry before transitioning to AST.

Rev. Ismael Ruiz-Millán, MDiv, is director of the Hispanic House of Studies, global education, and intercultural formation at Duke Divinity School. He is an ordained elder in the North Carolina Conference of the United Methodist Church. He has taught pastors and church leaders on pastoral care, Latin American Christianity, and mission as well as seminars and workshops on cultural humility, leadership, and the Latinx experience in the United States.

Rev. Jennie Lee Salas is associate director in the field education office at Princeton Theological Seminary and parish associate at Iglesia Presbiteriana Nuevas Fronteras. She received her MDiv from Princeton Theological Seminary and her MSW from Rutgers University. She has been involved in the church for more than thirty-five years in various ministerial leadership roles. Her work continues to be part of community organizing and building spaces for courageous dialogue.

Rev. Cody J. Sanders, PhD, is pastor to Old Cambridge Baptist Church in Cambridge, Massachusetts, where he also serves as American Baptist chaplain to Harvard University and adviser for LGBTQ+ Affairs in the Office of Religious, Spiritual, & Ethical Life at the Massachusetts Institute of Technology. He is the author of several books including *A Brief Guide to Ministry with LGBTQIA Youth* (2017).

Rev. Axel Schoeber, DMin, PhD, is lead pastor at West Vancouver Baptist Church in West Vancouver, British Columbia. He is also a Reformation-era historian and has taught extensively in online theological education, publishing several articles on the subject.

Rev. Lia Scholl is pastor of Wake Forest Baptist Church in Winston-Salem, North Carolina. She has been a minister for twenty years, working in traditional churches and organizations advocating with and for sex workers, drug users, and returning citizens. She's the author of *I Heart Sex Workers* (2013). Originally from Alabama, she earned her MDiv at Beeson Divinity School at Samford University. Lia is married to Drew McCarthy and enjoys being a stepmother to Emma.

John Senior directs the Wake Forest School of Divinity's art of ministry program, which includes its field education curriculum. His research and teaching focus on pastoral formation for ministry, field-based learning, ministry leadership in both ecclesial and public settings, and the role of theological education in preparing leaders for a wide variety of institutional contexts. Trained in Christian ethics and the sociology of religion, Senior also is interested in political theology and ethics and Earth-centered approaches to ministry and the moral life. Senior is an ordained teaching elder in the Presbyterian Church (USA).

Rev. Allison St. Louis, PhD, serves as affiliate faculty, consultant, and spiritual director at Virginia Theological Seminary, Alexandria, Virginia. She also serves as a clinical psychologist and spiritual director in private practice in Hellam, Pennsylvania.

Trudy Hawkins Stringer, assistant professor of the practice of ministry at Vanderbilt Divinity School, teaches in the area of theological field education. She works with students to shape theology in the midst of on-the-ground practice. Through the privilege of teaching and learning with students and their communities, Trudy has developed a deep interest in the intersections of embodiment, gender, race, and justice-making in community through the lens of faith.

Rev. Dr. Geoff Vandermolen has served as a pastor for more than twenty years in the Christian Reformed Church, both as a church planter and as an established church pastor. He currently serves on the faculty of Calvin Theological Seminary (Grand Rapids, Michigan) as director of vocational formation and codirector of the doctor of ministry program. He has been married to Kristin for twenty-seven years, and together they have two great kids.

Made in the USA
Las Vegas, NV
12 August 2021

28045531R00121